D1480366

NASSER
MY HUSBAND

NASSER
MY HUSBAND

Tahia Gamal Abdel Nasser

Translated by
Shereen Mosaad

Edited by
Tahia Khaled Abdel Nasser

Foreword by
Hoda Gamal Abdel Nasser

The American University in Cairo Press
Cairo   New York

This English translation first published in 2013 by
The American University in Cairo Press
113 Sharia Kasr el Aini, Cairo, Egypt
420 Fifth Avenue, New York, NY 10018
www.aucpress.com

Exclusive distribution outside Egypt and North America by I.B. Tauris & Co Ltd., 6 Salem Road,
London, W2 4BU

Dar el Kutub No. 22319/12
ISBN 978 977 416 611 2

Dar el Kutub Cataloging-in-Publication Data

    Abdel Nasser, Tahia Gamal
        Nasser: My Husband / Tahia Gamal Abdel Nasser.—Cairo: The American University in
    Cairo Press, 2013.
            p.   cm.
            ISBN 978 977 416 611 2
        1. Abdel Nasser, Gamal (president), 1918–1970
        2. Egypt – History, 1919–1952
        3. Egypt – History, 1952–1970
            962.053

1 2 3 4 5   17 16 15 14 13

Designed by Adam el-Sehemy
Printed in Egypt

Contents

CONTENTS

CONTENTS

Foreword

Hoda Gamal Abdel Nasser

After my father's funeral period, which lasted forty days, as was the custom, my mother Tahia found herself in a difficult situation: the house had been full of mourners from Egypt, the Arab world, and foreign countries, who had come to express their deepest sympathy and share the family's sorrow (I still have the funeral notes and letters of condolence from statesmen and friends); now each one of us returned to his or her work and family. But fortunately for Tahia, her eldest son Khaled, who was still a student in the Department of Engineering at Cairo University, and her youngest son Abdel Hakim, who was still at school, were living at home. Abdel Hamid was a student at the Naval Academy in Alexandria and would come to Cairo at the end of every week. My sister Mona worked at Dar al-Ma'arif publishing house, and I had been my father's secretary since September 1969. It was then that President Sadat said to me: "My daughter, I would be happy if you worked with me." I thanked him, and preferred to work as a researcher at *al-Ahram* newspaper with my father's friend Mohamed Hassanein Heikal.

There were no problems in my mother's life in general, and she had no wishes. After Gamal Abdel Nasser, her life was devoted to family, friends, and acquaintances who had strong attachments to my father and thus never left her alone. And at that most difficult of moments, her grandchildren Hala and Gamal were the joy in her life.

During the eleven-year rule of President Sadat, relations were good until the policy change that followed the 6 October 1973 War, when the regime turned against the principles and policies of Gamal Abdel Nasser, and attacks were launched against him in the media seeking to distort his legacy. An organized campaign of character assassination began after 1973, extended to the Camp David Accords, and lasted until Sadat's assassination on 6 October 1981.

The sorrow my mother endured at that time cannot be forgotten, and what shocked her the most was that the campaign had been launched in the presidency of Anwar Sadat, Gamal's friend. On many occasions, she visited me in tears after reading a newspaper article full of allegations against her beloved husband, and she would say to me: "Now I feel better. On the way, people in their cars waved at me in solidarity: to tell me to carry on and endure, we are with you." Gamal Abdel Nasser left Tahia an exceptional legacy—the love, appreciation, and respect of the people.

Neither Sadat nor Mubarak placed any limits on the activities or movements of the family, because none of its members pursued any political activity or ambitions, and Gamal's children remained distant from politics in spite of the many opportunities to become politically involved.

One year after my father's passing, I began the project of collecting, archiving, and publishing his papers, photographs, and speech and film recordings. I enrolled in the PhD program in the Department of Political Science and Economics at Cairo University, having decided to obtain a PhD in the philosophy of political science in order to attain the level of training necessary to undertake such a project. I defended my dissertation at Cairo University in 1985, and became an assistant professor in my department.

I began to consider the traditional idea of establishing a foundation in my father's name, but could not because of the lack of funds needed for such a venture. After that, I began collecting his speeches, with the aim of transcribing the recordings for the sake of accuracy. Abdel Hakim had already requested them in Sadat's era, but to no avail. In 1995, I met the minister of information, Safwat al-Sherif, who granted permission for me to record all the television and radio archives on the President, and my joy was unparalleled.

In my documentary project, as I worked from home, I was helped by the considerable advancement that took place in electronic media, in terms of efficiency and scope. With the advent of the Internet, I was able to establish the foundation that I had envisioned, on the digital archive www.nasser.org, hosted by the Alexandria Library, in 2005. This includes an extensive collection on my father's life and work: private papers, letters, communiqués, official documents, presidential decrees, photographs, documentary films, texts and sound files of speeches, coins, and medals. I continue to add historical documents to this digital collection. So finally, material on the life and work of Gamal Abdel Nasser is now available to any researcher and everyone who wishes to consult his legacy and this major period in Egypt's modern history.

The publication of my mother's memoir was delayed because the prevailing political mood was hostile to Nasser in Egypt under the Sadat regime and to a lesser extent during Mubarak's rule. Two months before the 25 January Revolution of 2011, we decided to publish the memoir, as a different mood was just beginning to form. That was the first Arabic edition; now it has been translated into English.

Translated by Tahia Khaled Abdel Nasser

Prologue

DEARLY DEPARTED

The date is 24 September 1973. In four days' time it will be three years since the death of Gamal Abdel Nasser—the great leader, my beloved husband. There is not a minute that passes when I do not feel the sadness, when every moment I lived with him is not in my mind's eye: his voice, his always radiant image, his humanity, his struggles, his challenges, his words, his speeches.

With the memories come the tears; even when I laugh I feel the tears constantly choking me.

I lived with Gamal Abdel Nasser for eight years before the Revolution, and for eighteen years after it began on 23 July 1952.

We were married on 29 June 1944, which means I lived with him for twenty-six years and three months, and now I am living and counting the days since his death.

There were two phases of my life with Gamal Abdel Nasser, one before the Revolution and one after, and now I am living the third phase to which he is not witness—how difficult it is; a cruel phase in all ways.

It is only him I miss. I was not affected by those eighteen years: to me he was only my beloved husband; he was not the President of the Republic or I the President's wife.

The long years I lived before the death of the President (I was used to saying 'the President,' and I feel that I can say nothing else, so I will continue to use it) were filled with surprises and events. But to me they were not difficult years; I was happy and joyful. I sometimes laughed in the face of impending adversity, and thanked God when it passed.

The first time I thought about writing about my life with Gamal Abdel Nasser was while he was in Syria during the union in 1959, attending the celebrations. I spent nearly three years constantly writing about both the past and current events, and one day I asked myself: "Why am I writing?" But the President was aware of and welcomed the endeavor.

I changed my mind, telling myself that I did not want to continue writing, and I disposed of all my work. I informed the President and he sorrowfully asked me why I had done that. I told him that I was happy as I was and did not want to write anything down. I said, "Maybe the facts I am writing about could be embarrassing to some people." He told me, "Do what makes you feel more comfortable." I had written about events and situations that I had seen unfold in our house, what I used to hear and witness, and what the president told me. So I decided never to write and said to him, "What business is it of mine!" And we laughed.

Last year, however, I decided to start again, knowing full well how sorry he was that I had not continued to write and had abandoned my earlier writing. I live now as if he is by my side; I only take actions he would have approved of. If I thought he would not have approved of my writing, I would not have written a word.

I started to write and live with my memories, but I found myself profoundly affected both emotionally and physically; my tears flowed and my health waned, and so I put down my pen and decided to simply wait until the time came to lie down by his side. And for the second time I disposed of what I had written. But on the third anniversary of his death, I found myself again eager to write. So, let me bear whatever pain it brings me now that I am talking about the third stage of my life, after the death of the President.

I live in Manshiyat al-Bakri, in the house of President Gamal Abdel Nasser, with my youngest son Abdel Hakim, a student at the Faculty of Engineering at Cairo University, who is now eighteen years and eight months old. He is the one who encouraged me to write and insisted that he longed to know everything about his great father.

Hakim has asked for the tapes of his father's speeches to listen to, for he did not have the opportunity to hear all the words of his father when he was a child, and some dated back to before he was born. He tried to get them himself; he first asked the prime minister, whose son was his friend, and was given a promise. He asked the president, whom he met with personally, and was also given a promise. And he asked me to buy the blank tapes to be copied by the broadcasting company, and I told him I was willing to pay any price. Finally, I met the minister of culture by mere coincidence and asked him about the tapes. He told me, "No one has requested anything from me," and he promised to look into the matter. I hope by the Grace of God that the tapes reach my son Abdel Hakim soon.[1]

Since the death of the President, I have found the dear citizens of this country honoring his memory, for Gamal Abdel Nasser is in their hearts. The telegrams, letters, poetry, prose, and books I receive from the dear sons of Egypt, from the Arab world in general, and from the West, and the invitations I get to visit heads of friendly nations and their visits to me when they are in Egypt, or the visits of their representatives and ministers, are all proof of this appreciation and loyalty.

When I go out, I see the looks of the people around me: some wave their hands in greeting, others look at me with sadness, and I

---

1   Abdel Hakim Abdel Nasser never received the tapes during Sadat's rule, but Hoda Abdel Nasser received them during Mubarak's presidency.

see the loyalty and acknowledgment in their eyes. How thankful I am to them. At times I am in the car with tears in my eyes, and a car passes by me and the people wave. How grateful I feel as I pass by the Gamal Abdel Nasser Mosque in Manshiyat al-Bakri.

I see all this as a greeting to Gamal Abdel Nasser, and any acknowledgment I receive is for him.

Early Years

GAMAL PROPOSES TO TAHIA

Let me now talk of my memories with Gamal Abdel Nasser: firstly, how he made my acquaintance and how he married me.

My family had a longstanding friendship with his. He used to visit us with his uncle and his aunt, who was a friend of my mother, and meet with my second brother, and at times he would see me and greet me. When he decided to marry he sent his uncle and aunt to ask for my hand in marriage. At the time, he was a captain in the armed forces. My brother—who, after my father's death, considered himself to be my guardian—said that I could not marry before my older sister. Gamal was of the same opinion; he said that he did not intend us to be married until after my sister was married, which happened one year later.

After that, my brother still did not agree to me getting married. The tradition in our family allowed me to refuse a suitor, but did not allow me to choose one. In my heart I knew that I wanted to marry Captain Gamal Abdel Nasser.

A few months later, my mother passed away. I then lived alone with my brother, since my second brother had gone to live abroad.

My brother had taken over the management of the enterprises of my late father, who had been affluent, which made him a wealthy man.

He was cultured and educated, holding a degree in commerce, and he worked in trade and on the stock exchange. He was strict at home and extremely conservative, but outside he had his own private life.

I lived alone with my brother for some months, my sisters visiting me occasionally. On one of my sister's visits, she told us that the uncle and aunt of Captain Gamal Abdel Nasser had visited her and asked about me, saying that Gamal wanted to marry Tahia, and requesting that she broach the subject with my brother. My brother now welcomed the idea: "We are old friends and more than family"—and he set a date to receive them, 14 January 1944.

I met Gamal with my brother, arranged for the engagement to be held within a week, and agreed on the dowry and all the arrangements of a wedding. Obviously, all details were discussed after I had sat with them for a while in the salon and then excused myself. On 21 January 1944, my brother held a dinner party; we invited our relatives, and Gamal's father, uncle, and aunt attended. He put the wedding ring on my finger, telling me that he had inscribed the date of 14 January. He meant the first day that he had come to visit me, adding that on that day he had not come to see if the bride appealed to him, as was the custom in those days: he had already made his decision—this is what I understood from his words.

My brother had decided that the marriage ceremony would take place on the same day as the wedding, after our home was ready. [2] Gamal could visit me once a week in the presence of my sister or my brother himself, and, since my brother was usually busy and rarely at home, my sister usually acted as chaperone. Gamal agreed to my brother's terms and asked if we could go out together accompanied by my sister and her husband, and my brother agreed.

I noticed that he did not enjoy just going out for a walk or sitting somewhere; he preferred the cinema or theater, especially Naguib

---

2   In Arab Muslim culture there are two, often separate, parts to a marriage: the marriage contract and the wedding celebrations.

al-Rihani.[3] I had only seen a very few shows and so everything for me was new. We went out by taxi and usually had lounge or baignoire seats at the theater or cinema, and we would have dinner at home on our return.

Five and a half months later, on 29 June 1944, I was married to Captain Gamal Abdel Nasser.

My brother held the wedding for us. After the ceremony, I went with Gamal to have our wedding photograph taken by Arman the photographer. It was the first time for me to go out with him without my sister and her husband. We filled a cart with flowers as a background to the picture. This photograph was published after his death in *al-Ahram*'s special pictorial issue.

We went back home for the wedding celebrations and at one in the morning the guests all left. We were sitting in the salon, just him and me, when my brother entered looking at his watch, saying, "It is now one o'clock. You will stay another hour, until two." And he looked so deeply affected that Gamal told him, "We will stay with you until you tell us to go home!"

At two o'clock my brother hugged me and wept and told us to leave. As for me, a tear rolled down my cheek, which greatly affected Gamal.

I remember a time, many years later, when we were sitting for lunch at the dining table with our children, remembering my brother, and Gamal laughingly said, "The only man in the world whose conditions I accepted was Abdel Hamid Kazem." And we all laughed.

OUR FIRST HOME

I had not seen the apartment before, or the furnishings. It was on the third floor. We went up the first two flights and then he carried me up the remaining floor to our home. The apartment took up the whole

---

3   Naguib al-Rihani (1890–1949) was a celebrated actor, writer, and founder of theatrical troupes who contributed to the development of Egyptian theater through a form of comedy of manners that examined contemporary social and political issues.

floor; it had three doors: the first to the dining room, the second to the sitting room, and the third, middle, door to the salon. We found the whole apartment lit: all five rooms. Gamal took my hand and led me into all the rooms; I loved it all and was very happy. I had spent my inheritance from my father, an amount not comparable to my brother's wealth, on setting up the house. I started my life with my beloved husband in great happiness. We lived simply, off Gamal's salary. I had left my brother and his affluence, and I missed nothing, not even the telephone. I never felt that I was in need of anything or had forgotten anything. The first time I left the house was three days after our marriage; we went to the photographer Arman to see our wedding photographs. There were two pictures, and Gamal told me to choose the one I liked. The one I chose is hanging in the house at Manshiyat al-Bakri with our children's photographs today.

EARLY MARRIED LIFE

We were on a long holiday, as Gamal worked as a teacher at the Military Academy. He told me that he would start studying at the beginning of November to prepare for the entrance exam to the Staff Officers Academy.

We stayed for two weeks in Cairo, where we were like any other couple, going out and receiving guests, most of whom were relatives coming to congratulate us. I noticed that when we went out he pre-ferred going to the cinema, just like me.

After this we traveled to Alexandria, where we stayed for another two weeks. At the time, there were many British people in Alex-andria, as the war was not yet over. Places were crowded and the streets were dark due to the air raids. I remember once, we were walking on the Corniche, along the seafront. It was dark and I was afraid, seeing all the British around me. Gamal laughed and said, "Why are you afraid?"

When we returned to Cairo, we were still on holiday and we used to go out together. We occasionally visited my sisters. My sister who married before me was in the hospital after giving birth to Laila, her daughter. Twenty years later, the President and Field Marshal Amer attended her wedding and were witnesses to the marriage ceremony.

My visits to my sisters were rare, as they lived in Giza, and although my brother's residence was not as far as Giza, he was rarely at home.

None of Gamal's officer friends visited us. He said that he had told them that he would not be calling anyone during his holiday. He spent all his time with me. The only friend he mentioned to me was Abdel Hakim Amer, who had been posted with him at Manqabad, his first posting after his graduation from the Military Academy. He said that Amer was currently in al-Minya with his wife on holiday. Gamal had also told him that he would only visit him after the holidays.

The holiday ended and the officers' visits began. Abdel Hakim Amer came back from al-Minya and visited Gamal at home.

Gamal did not favor mixed social interaction, with friends and officers bringing their wives and all of us sitting together. If a friend visited with his wife, he would greet them alone and lead the lady to the salon. He would then come to me in my room and tell me, "There is a lady in the salon, receive and entertain her until her husband's visit is over." I would usually not see the husband at all; the lady would leave the salon, the man would leave through the sitting room, and they would go out together. If Gamal wanted me to visit the lady myself, he would ask me to go alone, and, thus, the next time she visited me, she would also come alone, and her husband would then visit Gamal alone after that.

Captain Gamal Abdel Nasser was a teacher at the Military Academy, and he had shift duties; he had to spend the night at the Academy once a week, sometimes more depending on the shift schedule. When he went to the Academy in the morning, he would sometimes leave so early that he needed to have a small flashlight in his pocket; even though there was a light on the stairs he would still use his flashlight. He would insist that I should not get up or prepare anything for him, to such an extent that I used to feel that my getting up might annoy him. He would say, "I will have breakfast at the Academy." At other times he would leave late, just before eight, as the Academy was so close to our house.

He was a very organized, independent man and did not welcome assistance. When he came home he would carefully put his suit on the coat-hanger and place it in the closet. He also had a coat stand in the room that still exists in its place today. I used to offer my help, but he never accepted.

PREPARING FOR THE ENTRANCE EXAM
TO THE STAFF OFFICERS ACADEMY

At the beginning of November, Gamal started studying. He would come back from the Academy at around one in the afternoon or later, and we would have lunch at 1:30. At times he would go back to the Academy and other days he would stay at home, depending on the teaching schedule.

The study schedule would last from three until just after sunset, when he would receive guests, mostly his officer friends. They would not all come together; one would come and another would leave, or two or three might come together. After that he would stay at home or go out with one or two of his guests. I began to recognize the voices: I knew Abdel Hakim Amer's voice; he had a very particular way of speaking and a distinctive laugh. Whether Gamal came home early or took his time, he was never unduly late.

Gamal studied in the dining room. He would put his files, papers, and reference books on the table and would organize the files he was working on diligently. I noticed he wrote a lot in his diaries. We would have dinner together if he had not gone out or had come home early.

When the exam time approached, Gamal would study till morning, having just a sandwich while working. He told me that the entrance exam to the Staff Officers Academy was not easy; getting through the acceptance exam was more difficult than the studies at the Academy itself. This was because the subjects were all in English and the instructors were all British. Every year a large number of officers applied and only a very few passed, for the exam was in two rounds. Those who passed the first exam would go on to the second, and only those who passed the second would be accepted into the Academy. The first exam was in May, in six months' time.

During these periods of study, Gamal often received his officer friends. I noticed that at times he would receive a guest, letting him in through the salon door and seating him in the dining room, and then he would receive another guest and let him in through another door to a different room. He would not sit with guests simultaneously or meet them together, and each would leave alone. Some of his colleagues would sit and study with him in the dining room. At times, I would hear raised voices discussing the material they were studying, and I could always hear the paper puncher when Gamal was organizing his files. Abdel Hakim Amer was one of the most frequent guests and study partners at that time.

We would go out together once a week, mostly to the cinema. The season of new films had started at the Metro and the Rivoli. Gamal would book the tickets in advance so as to choose the best seats. I never needed to ask him to go out; he always had our outing planned and he would tell me what time he wanted me to be ready. This continued until May. Gamal entered the exam and passed, coming in fourth place, but, as he had told me, this was just the first round.

THE HATED *MURASALA* SYSTEM

When I felt the symptoms of pregnancy, Gamal took me to a well-known doctor and came with me on each of the monthly visits prescribed by the doctor. At the time, it was common practice among officers to have a soldier on duty, under the officer's command. These soldiers were known as *murasala*. Gamal hated this system, believing that at times it was abused by the officers, who treated this soldier like a houseboy. He felt there was a great injustice in this practice, since the soldier could not complain or revolt against any mistreatment, nor could he leave the house and quit the job. I fully agreed with Gamal on this issue.

I prepared his dress suit myself, giving the stars and buttons to the maid to polish, then I would fix them onto the suit with the special copper pins. I remember that on one of Gamal's visits to me before our marriage I had asked him about the stars on his shoulder pads and how they were fixed on, and he had laughingly twisted one round and let me in on the secret.

When our maid traveled to her village for a holiday, Gamal brought in a *murasil* to serve in the house. These young men came from very poor families, often farmers who worked for the rich landowners, and could not pay twenty Egyptian pounds to avoid military service. He informed me that the man would be doing only his personal things and shopping for what was needed in the house. I happily complied with Gamal's instructions at all times, fully convinced of his opinions.

Gamal continued to study for the second, December, exam. The visits of his officer friends and others continued in the same pattern. Sometimes there was only one visitor and at other times the salon would be filled with his friends, never arriving or leaving at the same time. Once again, among the study partners who worked with him in the dining room, Abdel Hakim Amer was the most frequent, and he once brought his wife with him and we sat together while the men studied. In the last days before the exam, an officer called Zakaria Mohieddin joined Gamal in the dining room. I could hear him discussing the material they were studying, asking questions and repeating concepts. I got to recognize his voice from the way he used to deliberate each point. Gamal told me that his father owned land, that he was not married, and that he drove his own new car.

Out of the many applicants taking the exam, only a few passed. I do not remember the exact number, but they did not exceed thirty. Gamal, Abdel Hakim, and Zakaria all passed the exam.

HODA'S BIRTH

I was at the end of my pregnancy and when, late one night, I started going into labor, Gamal took me to the hospital and stayed with me until I gave birth to our daughter Hoda at eight in the morning of 12 January 1946. He had not informed the family during the night, but once the baby was born, he told me he would telephone my sister and then go home to rest.

Around that time, Gamal joined the Staff Officers Academy for two years of study. The hours of studying decreased and the visitors increased; they would come at any time after he returned from the Academy. They would come before, or after, or even during lunch. We would be sitting having our meal and a guest would arrive. Gamal would leave the table, telling me to finish my lunch and he would eat later. The guests never stayed long, but Gamal was a light eater and never came back to finish his lunch.

At times, he would rest in the bedroom after lunch, but this never lasted long. It was never more than half an hour before a guest would arrive, whom he would meet in the salon, followed by another, then another. Sometimes he would leave the house with one of his friends, coming back alone or with someone else.

Until this point, I had not noticed anything strange or clandestine. He would at times bring guns to the house, which I myself placed in the cupboard, not giving it a second thought since he was, after all, an officer.

One night at around ten he told me he was going out and would not be back till dawn. He told me he would knock on the door, and showed me how he would knock three times for me to wake up and open the door. He also told me that he might have people with him for a meeting. I left the bedroom door open so that I would hear him when he came back. This was repeated more than once, but I was happy and content, seeing the love and devotion in his eyes. He often played with Hoda, our daughter, and would fondly carry her into the salon to meet his guests for a few minutes. All I wished was to be able to do the utmost for his comfort.

GAMAL THE MAN

Toward the end of 1946, Abdel Hamid, my brother, fell ill with tuberculosis and was confined to bed. Since my second brother had returned from abroad he had lived in his own apartment and, consequently, Abdel Hamid lived alone. I was in my second pregnancy at the time, and our visits to him were few, but once he fell ill Gamal began to visit him frequently. He would come home and tell me my brother's news, trying to ease my worries. My relatives visited my brother rarely and with great caution, often standing at the door to the room. Gamal told me that he never felt afraid when visiting a sick person and was never worried about being infected, that this was inhuman.

My brother was admitted to hospital for surgery on his lungs. The day he left the hospital, Gamal went to visit him and stayed until after three in the morning. When he returned home he told me that my brother had not been feeling well and had difficulty breathing, and my sisters, who were at his side at the time, got up and left. Gamal felt he could not leave him alone in such a state and, even though my brother urged him to go home, he insisted on staying. At around three, my brother claimed he was feeling better and would have a glass of milk, and Gamal waited until he felt it was safe to leave him before coming home. He was astonished at how my sisters could act in this way and leave Abdel Hamid. When my brother recovered, he visited our sisters and told them that the person he loved the most and held most dear was Gamal Abdel Nasser, that he was the most humane person he had met in his life, and that he loved him more than he loved them.

MONA'S BIRTH

An officer friend and his wife visited us during the last days of my pregnancy and I received them with Gamal in the salon. They asked what we would call the baby if it was a boy and Gamal answered, "Khaled." The officer was Tharwat Okasha. A few days later I gave birth to our daughter Mona.

THE FIRING OF UNLOADED GUNS

Things went on as before—guests coming at all times and asking about him in his absence, and him going out and coming back home to meet guests or accompanied by a guest who sat with him in the salon, sometimes studying for the Academy.

One day, my sister and her husband visited me and, as we sat in the sitting room, we could hear Gamal and his guests in the salon. We heard a clicking sound and my brother-in-law exclaimed that it was the sound of an empty gun being tested. I quickly remembered the sound of the paper puncher and told my brother-in-law that it was Gamal organizing his papers and files. In fact, it was the sound of guns.

One night I was in bed putting baby Mona to sleep. The light was off and the door to the room open. Someone knocked on the front door and the *murasil* soldier found a man asking for Gamal. When he informed him that he was not at home, the man left without leaving his name. Through the open door of my bedroom I had seen the man's face and recognized him. When Gamal returned, I told him that Aziz al-Masri had been to visit him. When he asked me if I was sure, I told him that he was a well-known adventurer and I had seen many pictures of him in the newspapers before our marriage. Gamal went straight out and when he came back he told me that he had gone to Aziz al-Masri and told him that I had recognized him. The man had confirmed that he had indeed visited Gamal and not left his name.

I still did not understand anything. I only knew there were guns of different sizes in the house—more than one—and the visit of Aziz al-Masri was a confidential matter that no one should know of but myself.

To Palestine

Gamal completed his studies at the Staff Officers Academy and graduated in May 1948. Two days before graduation, he asked me to prepare his suit for him and to sew on a red badge below the military badge, which I happily did. Captain Gamal Abdel Nasser graduated, and I proudly congratulated him with love.

Two days later, he asked me to pack his bags because he was traveling to Palestine to fight. It was a surprise to me, and I cried. When he asked me why I was crying, I told him, "How can I not cry when you are going away to war? And I used to cry when you only left the house!" After packing, I saw him put a first-aid kit in the bag, trying not to let me see it.

The war started on 15 May 1948, and on 16 May at seven in the morning, Gamal left the house. I tearfully watched him go down the stairs to the jeep waiting outside, and his brothers came to bid him farewell.

I was alone with my daughters, Hoda, aged two years and five months, and Mona, aged one year and four months. The maid had traveled to her village two weeks earlier, and Gamal had told me to be very careful about my choice of new maid, preferably someone my sisters knew.

The wife of Hamdi Ashour, one of the officers who stayed in Cairo and did not travel to Palestine, used to visit me and they used to send me their *murasil* soldier to do my shopping every day.

Gamal's brothers returned to Alexandria, where they were at university, and his father came and stayed a month with me. After that his brothers used to come and visit me during their holidays.

Nothing mattered to me but the news of the war and news of Gamal. I waited for his letters, which I joyfully received only to start worrying after reading them and wondering what could have happened to him after sending them. I would often sit alone and cry.

In a letter dated 18 May 1948, he wrote: "I hope you and our dear daughters are well; as for me, nothing is cause for concern."

22 May 1948: "I am well and only concerned about your comfort and well-being and wish to see you soon in the best of spirits."

24 May 1948: "I am writing to you with no concern but your well-being, and I hope your sister has provided a maid for you. Take good care of Mona and Hoda."

9 June 1948: "We will meet soon after the victory, God willing."

He asked me in a letter to go to my brother's house at a certain time so that he could call me. He called and asked about Hoda and Mona, and told me that he was well and that he would call me the following week at the same time. I went then and he called, and he told me, "I'll call you every week."

I went the next week and waited, but he did not call. Then I received a letter in which he told me that he had had no opportunity to call because they were moving around, and he gave me another time for a telephone call. Again I waited for his call, but it did not come, and in a letter he told me he had been too busy.

In a letter dated 23 July 1948, he wrote: "I miss our home greatly and will come home soon. By the way, on 20 Ramadan I will be promoted."

In another letter, he told me he would be taking three days' leave. I was beside myself with joy. He came home, having been away for three and a half months.

A BULLET WOUND

I saw a fresh wound and stitching on the left side of his chest and asked him about it. He told me it was nothing, just a small wound, and fell silent. While I was unpacking his bag, I found a handkerchief, vest, and shirt heavily soiled with blood. I turned to him for an explanation. He looked at me and said that he was shot while in the army jeep; the bullet hit the metal on the front of the car—only a few centimeters thick, but it served to slow the bullet down—and only a fragment of it hit him, close to the heart. He was hospitalized for a couple of days. Showing me the fragment, he told me he would keep it as a memento along with the clothes that showed where it had entered.

Gamal stayed for the three days, receiving members of the family, and we went out to the cinema once. I wept when he left, but he told me he would write me letters and visit me once a month. He did come the following month for three days' leave, from 14 to 17 September, when he returned to Palestine.

THE SIEGE OF AL-FALUJA

Abdel Hakim Amer returned from Palestine to Cairo. He had also been wounded, in the hand, and had taken leave. I went to pay a visit to his family and for the first time I met him, and we shook hands. He told me that Gamal was fine and in good health, and would be coming back shortly for a holiday. We were approaching the Great Feast and I waited for Gamal, but the feast came and went, and Gamal had not come for leave. I was still receiving letters, but they came less frequently, and he did not mention when he would be coming for a holiday. I was reading the newspapers diligently and listening to the radio. I was getting very worried. I told my sister to ask her husband for news, and he informed her that the army had moved to a remote location, not within reach of any trains.

Before leaving for Palestine, Gamal had given me checks so as to be able to cash his salary from Bank Misr, and then in a letter dated

17 October 1948 he told me that he had wired money to my account in al-Ahly Bank, which I could use at the beginning of each month. He told me not to worry and to concern myself only with the well-being of Hoda and Mona, and that was his wish.

On the way to the bank one morning, I met a neighbor of one of my sisters who asked me if my husband was still a prisoner of war. Shocked, I managed only to reply that he had not been taken prisoner, only that he was stationed in a remote area.

I remained at home in a state of extreme worry. My downstairs neighbor was the daughter of the Chief of General Staff of the army at the time, Osman al-Mahdi Pasha. I told her about Gamal and she offered to ask her father. A few days later, she knocked on my door in the early morning, carrying a magazine. She showed me a picture of Major Gamal Abdel Nasser among a number of officers in al-Faluja, and so I came to know of the Faluja siege.[4]

Every now and then I would ask my neighbor to inquire about the soldiers in al-Faluja from her father. She told me that her father would soon be visiting her, and she asked me to join them and ask him myself. She was kind and considerate, and I remember her fondly to this day, Nadia al-Mahdi. I used to visit her only rarely, while she asked about me almost daily. She always used to tell me that since I was alone I should also visit her, but I told her that she was busy with her husband and children and I did not want to intrude. One day she invited me to attend her son's birthday and bring Hoda and Mona with me. Only her younger sister was with them, and so I agreed. There I met her father, who told me that the soldiers in al-Faluja were fine and that they were being sent guns and ammunition, and would soon be home.

---

4 Al-Faluja was a Palestinian village that fell within the territory allotted to the Arabs under the 1947 UN Partition Plan. During the Palestine War of 1948, four thousand Egyptian troops, of which Gamal Abdel Nasser was deputy commander, were encircled by Israeli forces in al-Faluja. The siege lasted from October 1948 until February 1949, when an armistice agreement allowed the evacuation of the Egyptian column, and the area was transferred to Israeli control.

In a letter dated 21 November 1948, Gamal wrote: "Please don't worry about the infrequency of the letters. I send them when I can and when circumstances permit. They might be sporadic for the time being."

23 November 1948: "I hope we meet soon in the best possible circumstances. Please don't be worried; I always try to write to put your mind at ease. I have written you three letters, which I hope you have received. Anyway, don't expect regular letters these days. I have not received a letter from you for forty-five days due to the difficulty of them getting here, but I regularly receive news that you are well from Abdel Hakim."

26 November 1948: "I can receive news of you through Abdel Hakim. You can call his wife and let her know how you are, and Abdel Hakim calls me daily. I will not be able to receive letters from you for the time being, but I am well and there is no cause for concern."

14 January 1949: "I did not think we would be apart for all this time, but, still, I thank God. I am encouraged by your faith, and you should not worry and not be saddened by this separation. God willing, we will meet soon. I am fine and we shall forget this hardship and be together, my loved one, forever."

In another letter, he wrote: "I hope you take Hoda out regularly to the zoo and the fish garden. I hope you are always well and happy."

I went and visited my sister, who lives in Giza, close to the zoo, and I took Hoda and Mona. I had never been to the fish garden before, so I did not go there. Hoda had started to talk and had learned the names of two birds.

I hardly went out, remaining at home reading the newspapers and listening to the radio, praying that the siege in al-Faluja would end and Gamal would return safely.

My neighbor, Nadia al-Mahdi, often asked me to go out with her to the cinema, but I always declined. I was not really used to going out alone or with any of the ladies. I did not actually have any friends and my relations with all the officers' wives were limited, and they were all the same to me. I spent my free time knitting for

Hoda and Mona, and I started working on a pullover for Gamal, in light grey, his favorite color.

A letter arrived on 20 January 1949: "I will be seeing you very soon, God willing, before the beginning of February or at the latest during the first week of February. And we will be together for always. I think the first moment I see you again will be the happiest of my life. I hope the pullover is finished."

I understood then that my letter had reached him, and I was very happy that he would be home soon.

These are all parts of his letters to me from Palestine. They were forty-six letters in total, and I kept them all, with his signature at the bottom, which never changed.

I sat alone at night knitting after Hoda and Mona slept, remembering conversations with Gamal when we were engaged. I remembered him telling me about his travels; I had expected not to live much in Cairo when we got married and I was enthusiastic about traveling with him. I told myself, "Can it be that the first trip he takes after our marriage is to go to war? He is now under siege in al-Faluja and I do not know when it will end." In all the letters he sent me, he made me feel that he was safe and would return soon, and I thought perhaps he wanted to give me hope to lessen my sorrow in his long absence.

One day my neighbor told me that the landlady wanted me to leave the house because she planned on building an extra floor above our apartment. My neighbor was shocked at the landlady's request and asked her how I was expected to move house while my husband was away at war. The landlady suggested that I go and live with my brother. I told my neighbor that I would only leave the house when Gamal Abdel Nasser came back home, which would be soon.

Return from al-Faluja

A TELEPHONE CALL FROM ARISH

At the beginning of March 1949, Gamal telephoned and said he was in Arish, and asked me to go to my brother's house on the following day so that he could talk to me. I was elated that he was back and that we could talk. He asked about Hoda and Mona, and also told me that he wanted to speak to his father. So the next day his father came with me to my brother's house and spoke with Gamal. He told me that he would call me every day at eight in the morning until he returned to Cairo.

On 6 March 1949, Gamal returned from al-Faluja. My happiness was beyond words. His brothers came from Alexandria to welcome him home, and all the neighbors and shopkeepers in the district were waiting for him. Everyone had heard of al-Faluja and everyone wanted to welcome the soldiers back.

After resting for a short while, he rose and decided to get dressed in his regular clothes, saying that he had had enough of wearing his uniform. He asked about his new pullover that I had finished and put in the closet. It was the first item of clothing he wore upon his return. He went out to visit the barracks, promising to be back quickly.

He had been away for five months, and Hoda and Mona had changed: Mona had started to talk and Hoda had grown more eloquent.

We had many visitors, including relatives from Alexandria and Upper Egypt. The holiday was to be for one month. We often went out together to the cinema. We also went and spent the day at the agricultural exhibition and had lunch. We met an officer friend of Gamal's who had been married only two weeks before. He greeted us and said, "We are not alone on honeymoon; you are as well," and we all laughed.

MOVING TO A NEW HOUSE

In the last week of March, Gamal told me that an acquaintance of his, a high-ranking officer, had a villa in the Kubri al-Qubba area. He had built two floors above the original villa, and the second floor was empty and Gamal was thinking of renting it for us. I welcomed the idea, and he went with the officer to see it. He told me that it was satisfactory and that I should go and take a look, but I told him that I was fine with moving as long as he liked it. The area was known to be quiet and the second floor meant easy stairs. I had not mentioned the incident with our landlady; she had come to welcome him home, and had praised me highly to him.

At the end of March, the month that Gamal returned from al-Faluja, we left our house to move to Kubri al-Qubba. Our landlady, who was also a neighbor, came to bid us farewell in tears, saying that I had told her I would leave when Major Gamal Abdel Nasser returned from al-Faluja, and here I was leaving.

I went with Gamal, Hoda, and Mona to the new house that I had not previously seen, as had happened with my first home, and I liked it very much. The house was built with a basement and two stories for residence, and then a third floor. The new apartment had three doors, like the first, but it did not have a door that opened up to the dining room; the third door on the left opened into the kitchen. The house had five rooms, including a dining room and a salon with a door into the sitting room; both the dining room and the salon had a terrace that ran around the corner of the apartment, looking down on the main road of Heliopolis. I could see the bus and tram lines, and the bridge beside what was the military hospital at that time. I had a clear view of the main road, for we were the third villa on our street, and each had its own garden. The study opened out into the sitting room, without a door, and had a balcony and window onto the garden. On the other side of the apartment were two bedrooms.

Gamal used to tell me stories of his time at war and the siege of al-Faluja, and said, "There was a girl I used to talk to who reminded me of Hoda, and she was her age; one night I felt sad and wondered how Tahia was now, and Hoda and Mona, and I could not sleep." And he told me how bullets and bombs fell around him and God saved him; and how he used to read the Qur'an and pray; and how he used to send my letters with Arabs, and that each officer used to pay a sum that could amount to 50 Egyptian pounds for this.

IBRAHIM ABDEL HADI QUESTIONS GAMAL

The month's holiday ended and the Faluja veterans—three battalions—were relocated. Gamal was sent to Ismailiya. He told me that there were no family arrangements made in the Ismailiya barracks and that he would come and go between Ismailiya and Cairo on a weekly basis. He used to come to Cairo on Thursday and leave early on Saturday morning. I remained in Cairo and never visited Ismailiya.

We remained as such for nearly three months, during which time I was sickly because I was in the first months of pregnancy. Gamal told me he would take one month's leave, which made me very happy. On the first day of his holiday he went out early, came back before two, took off his clothes, and lay down on the bed in his pajamas, reading. Suddenly we heard someone outside, clapping their hands and asking for the residence of Major Gamal Abdel Nasser.

It was one of the officers. Gamal met him for a few minutes and then came into the room, put on his uniform, and told me he was going out. He told me not to wait for him and to have lunch with the children. I lunched with Hoda and Mona and the evening passed, but at around seven I started to worry. I did not understand what was happening around me; all I knew was that I must keep silent. I sat at the window, looking out onto the street, and waited.

I did not wait long; soon a large blue car pulled up in front of our house and Gamal got out, waiting for another passenger, Osman al-Mahdi Pasha, whom I recognized from our previous meeting. I quickly left my spot by the window in the dining room and went into the bedroom. Gamal and Osman Pasha sat for a while in the salon, and then Gamal came into the bedroom and asked me for the guns. He noticed how worried I looked and told me not to be afraid; that he would be back soon and would tell me everything after Osman Pasha had left. I told him that I had been watching from the window and that I had recognized him.

I had hidden the guns among the clothes in the cupboard. In the winter I hid them among the folded summer clothes and in the summer I hid them among the folded winter clothes; although he had never told me to, I always felt they should be hidden away and not seen by anyone but myself. When Osman Pasha left, Gamal came back to the room and told me that he had been called to a meeting with Prime Minister Ibrahim Abdel Hadi, in the presence of Osman Pasha. The prime minister, who had seemed very nervous and agitated, had interrogated him, and Gamal had answered all of his questions. When asked whether he had weapons, he had said that he had and had described them all. He was then asked to go home with Osman Pasha and hand over all the weapons in his possession. Gamal thought that he would be detained, but the prime minister, showing extreme annoyance, had told him to go home.

Gamal remained in Cairo for a month; we often went out, especially to the summer cinema in Heliopolis, sometimes taking Hoda and Mona. He met his guests, and sometimes went out with them or alone.

After the holiday, he was transferred from Ismailiya to the Administrative Affairs School in Cairo, where officers spent a specific time before being examined and then promoted. I was extremely happy that he was back in Cairo.

Gamal bought a black Austin that he paid for with the money saved from his salary during the war. Officers in action received double their salary. The money was not enough for the car, and so I contributed and we bought it together. A few days later he took Hoda, Mona, and me on a long drive to the Nile Barrages, where we had lunch.

Officers who were studying for the Staff Officers Academy exams used to come to the house to get Gamal's help in their studies. I used to hear them talking about the subjects, and he would give them his files, which he had prepared while studying himself for the same exams. He would tell me that he liked to offer his help to all those applying to the academy.

KHALED'S BIRTH

The months of my pregnancy passed and I would go to my doctor for the regular follow-up visits. In the last month of pregnancy, the doctor informed us that I would be giving birth in the new hospital he had built and he told us the approximate date of birth. He said he would book a room to be ready for me at that time and asked us if we knew of the new prices, as they had doubled since I had last given birth. Gamal asked him if the new prices applied to his old patients. The doctor answered that the new hospital was fully equipped with all modern equipment and means of comfort for the patient, and provided a high level of service, as well as foreign nurses. He added that there was also second-class accommodation available. Gamal quickly retorted, "So this means you go up and we go down?" After we left the clinic, Gamal told me that he would never go to that doctor again and would never enter his clinic or his hospital. He said that if I wished to go, I should ask one of my sisters to accompany me. I told him that there was no reason for me to go to that doctor and that I was most willing for him to find me another.

All through my pregnancy, I was praying for a boy: I was very eager to have a son. When I told Gamal of my feelings, he answered me, "God has his plans for the universe . . . do you want to organize it for Him? There is no difference between a boy and a girl." Still, I wanted a boy.

In the last week of my ninth month, we were in the car together with Hoda and Mona, who were all dressed up with ribbons in their hair. Gamal looked at them lovingly and told me, "Look how lovely they look. God willing, we will have three beautiful girls, with ribbons and all." So I said, "You still want a third girl?" And he answered, "I am happy with God's choice."

A few days later, my labor pains began at three in the morning and I woke Gamal up. He told me to get myself ready while he brought the car around to take me to the hospital in Dokki. In the car, the pains grew worse, but I hoped the baby would wait until morning. He asked me if I had thought of a name for our daughter and I told him, "I have not thought of a name, and I now have severe labor pains! Let me get through the pain first." It was Christmas Eve and people were still in the streets, celebrating.

We arrived at the hospital and were met by the nurses; the doctor showed up later, dressed in his evening clothes, and Khaled was born at five in the morning on 25 December 1949.

As soon as I regained consciousness, I asked the nurse if the baby was a boy or a girl. She asked me what children I already had and I told her I had two girls. She said, "It's a boy, Madam." I didn't believe her, thinking she was saying that because I told her I had two girls, until the doctor confirmed it, standing at the other end of the room, holding my baby.

The doctor went out to congratulate Gamal on his new son. Gamal came into the room and told me, "Now you have your son, Tahia." And he said, "Khaled." He had mentioned the name before Mona was born, but during this pregnancy he had not mentioned the name 'Khaled' or any other male names at all. I believe that he was trying to convince me that it would be a girl, knowing how much I wanted a boy, so that I would not be disappointed. In the morning he informed my sisters, who came to visit me. I asked about Abdel Hamid, my brother, who usually visited me in the hospital and bought me a gift, and they said that he sent his regards and that he was well.

THE PASSING OF MY BROTHER ABDEL HAMID

I stayed in the hospital until 4 January 1950. Gamal used to come and visit me each evening. Hoda and Mona were staying with my sister while I was in the hospital, and they came the day after the birth to see the baby. But my sisters did not come again after that, and neither did my brother. I was surprised that they didn't come, and thought that maybe the cold weather and the rain were keeping them away.

The day after I went back home, Gamal told me that he was invited out to lunch and that I should go ahead and eat with Hoda and Mona. I was annoyed by the timing of the invitation and would have preferred that Gamal stay with me on my first day home. When he returned, it was before suppertime and he asked for a light cheese snack. It seemed to me that he had not eaten out, and he said that he had a headache and was going to bed.

The next day was a Thursday and time for Umm Kulthum's monthly soirée. Gamal went out in the evening, but came home early. He told me he was tired and that he would not wait up to listen to Umm Kulthum, so I said I would join him, preferring not to stay up late during my first week back home.

I received the wife of the commander of the sixth battalion at al-Faluja as well as the wife of Hamdi Ashour, who came wearing mourning clothes. She apologized for coming in black, saying that she was paying her condolences at a nearby house and came to see me directly after. I was surprised by her actions and thought it would have been more appropriate if she had made a special visit to me. But I entertained her and served her sweets as is the custom, and showed her baby Khaled.

Twelve days passed and my sisters still had not visited me. I was resting in our bedroom with Gamal one afternoon, and I mentioned that, even though it was raining, it was strange that my sisters had not visited. He told me that Abdel Hamid was not well. He had caught a serious bout of influenza and, having weak lungs, had fallen very ill. I jumped up and started to get dressed to go and see him. Gamal said, "You know that we will each live only the days ordained to us by God." I quickly said, "He is dead then?" He replied, "Yes, he died the day after you came out of the hospital. I went and spent the whole day there, at the house."

I knew then that he had not been invited out to lunch, and that he had tried to act as normally as possible so that I would not notice. I cried and grieved deeply for Abdel Hamid. I also understood that the two ladies who had visited me were, in fact, paying their condolences and not congratulating me on the baby, for Gamal had strictly asked no one to mention the death of my brother to me. I also understood why he would not listen to Umm Kulthum on the radio, even though he usually loved to do so. I realized he had not listened to the radio at all during the past days, although I had listened to music. I recalled all that had happened around me and understood; he had also hidden the newspapers from me while I was busy with the baby.

Abdel Hamid had lost most of his money in the stock exchange and in the turbulence that had occurred in the market after the war, and so did not leave anything of his formerly large estate.

THE JEWISH DEAD IN AL-FALUJA

At the end of February 1950, Gamal told me that he would be traveling to Palestine for three days. The Egyptian government had agreed to show the Jews the places where their soldiers had fallen. He met again the Jewish officer, Cohen, whom he had met during the siege, when Gamal had refused to surrender and the three battalions had seen the siege through to the end. He told me that Cohen asked him about his children and that he had told him about Khaled, his two-month-old son.

Continual Meetings with the Officers

LIFE AT HOME IN KUBRI AL-QUBBA IN 1950

Visitors came constantly, most of them officers who spent some time with Gamal and then left; others—one or two—would stay late into the night, talking in low, muted tones. Some nights there would be a knock on the door after we had gone to bed and Gamal would rise and see his guest into the salon where they would talk for a while; some stayed till dawn. Some nights he had more than one visitor and on other nights he would get dressed and go out with the caller, even though the house had retired to bed. This was how it was. On the evenings that Gamal did not go out, we had dinner together at home.

On some nights, Gamal would receive one or more visitors and would ask me to make a light supper for them. I would go to bed and wake up every now and then to realize they were still with him outside, talking in the salon. Sometimes baby Khaled would wake during the night, and I would make him an herbal drink. I would then make coffee for Gamal and his guests, and knock on the dining-room door with the tray. Gamal would open the door and say, "Why did you trouble yourself making coffee?" I would tell him I had woken up with the baby and heard him with guests, and I knew how much he liked coffee. Often, in the mornings, I would see that he had made coffee during the late nights. He always told me not to tire myself and that making coffee was easy. Then he would thank me and I would go, and he would stay up until late at night, sometimes until dawn. This happened on most of the nights that Gamal was at home. During the day, even when he came back and had lunch with us, he could still go out at any time with one of the officers or on his own.

When Gamal was not home, the *murasil* soldier would open the door and take a message from the caller, who would most likely write down his name and the time he called on a piece of paper in what I called "military fashion": "1700 hours," and so on.

We had a piano in the sitting room, close to the bedroom door. We would place the pieces of paper left by callers—small snippets, not calling cards—on top of the piano, away from the curious little hands of Hoda and Mona. As soon as Gamal returned, he would look at the piano and take the papers, reading them before going into the bedroom.

At the times when the *murasil* was not in the house, I myself would open the door to callers asking for Major Gamal Abdel Nasser, and, likewise, I would be given the small pieces of paper with the names of the callers.

I did not talk to these callers, or even say "good morning" or "good evening." I hardly looked at them or saw their faces, except for a very few.

We would always have lunch together at 1:30 in the dining room if Gamal was home from work. Sometimes visitors started arriving while we were still having lunch and Gamal would ask me to take the girls and continue our lunch in the study, saying that he would sit with his guest and eat later. After this occurred many times, we bought a folding table and put it in the study for us to eat on, and we started having all our meals in the study, even breakfast, as Gamal sometimes received visitors before he went to work.

This eating arrangement continued for two years, until the Revolution.

We used to park the car in a lot in the street after ours. The area was very quiet, full of houses, with no apartment blocks, occupied mostly by officers since it was so close to the barracks. If I woke up during the night and Gamal was not home, I would lie awake and wait to hear his footsteps walking down the road from the lot. I would hear him come up the stairs. He sometimes had the key and would let himself in or, at other times, he would knock—his special three knocks that I knew so well—and I would open the door for him, and he would look into my eyes with love and appreciation. After that, he moved the car to a parking lot in our street, a few houses down from ours. The street was closed at that end by a wall that prevented access to Kubri al-Qubba Street from the Qubba Palace, and the cars parked up against the wall. When we parked in the next street, Gamal and I would walk home together, but after moving parking places, he would drop me off at home first, wait until I had gone into the building, and then go and park the car.

When I woke up during the night, I would hear the car passing in the street and I would see the light from the headlights. Then I would hear his footsteps approaching the house. One night he came back relatively early and knocked on the door. When I opened it and let him in, he said, "Have you had dinner?" I said, "Not yet." He told me that he had been out with Abdel Hakim and on their way back they had stopped at a restaurant to eat kebab. He asked the waiters to prepare another order to be ready to take home when they had finished eating. He said, "I asked myself how could I eat kebab and Tahia will just be eating cheese." Another time, he also brought me home a kebab dinner, but I had already eaten. The smell, however, was so tempting that I told him I would just taste some. Getting a plate and fork, I set to eating until he laughingly reminded me, "Tahia, don't forget that you have already had supper!"

We hardly ever had supper together because he was usually out of the house, and I had my meals alone, or sometimes I was too tired to eat and just went to bed. Gamal might have a light snack when he came back or nothing at all.

When he came back home early, he would always ask me if I had eaten, and if not we would eat together. If I did not really feel like eating, he would still ask me to eat with him.

Before the Revolution, our children were young and there was always one who was still a baby. The children's room was next to our bedroom, and I would hear the baby wake up in the night and cry, and I would get out of bed and go to his room to soothe him until he slept again. When the baby had a troublesome night and could not sleep, Gamal would come into the room and pick the baby up and walk around with him until he was calm and asleep. Whenever any of the children were sick, he would tell me in the morning that he would call for the doctor to come when he went to the office, since we didn't have a telephone at home. We dealt with a well-known doctor at the time who usually made his house call when Gamal was back home, and he would meet the doctor with me.

When one of the children had only a passing malady or we needed to change a feeding schedule or diet, we would visit the doctor at the clinic. Gamal would make an appointment and drive me there, and then pick me up after I had seen the doctor. I remember, once, Khaled became very sick when he was ten months old. Gamal was in the salon with one of his visitors and I knocked at the door. He opened it, looked at Khaled in my arms, and saw the worry on my face and contacted a doctor immediately, even though we could not find our regular doctor.

We often went out together to the cinema, sometimes well before the film was due to start, and we would park the car in a side street and walk along Fuad Street—now 26 July Street—and Qasr al-Nil Street. Once a photographer in Fuad Street took our photo and Gamal agreed to purchase it. I still have it with me today: it shows me walking by his side while he smoked a cigarette.

We once met Tharwat Okasha and his wife at the cinema and took them home to the barracks in Abbasiya on our way back. After that, it became a habit to pick them up on our way and take them home after the film.

Sometimes Gamal would tell me that he was going to Giza, and to prepare myself and the children to go to my sister's. We would go together in the car, and I would sit carrying the baby, while Hoda and Mona sat in the back. He would drop me off and then come and pick us up no later than nine or ten o'clock, and he would come upstairs first to say hello to my sister.

WEAPONS HIDDEN IN OUR HOUSE

Gamal used to go to Suez and Port Said once a month to train officers for two or three days, or sometimes he would be away for only one day.

We still had firearms in the house. The large machine guns were too big to be put in the cupboard, so I kept them in a corner in the dining room. They didn't stay for long, and I relaxed when they were taken away, only soon to be replaced by others.

Hoda and Mona were used to having the guns around and would get excited by any new ones. I kept the room locked and let them play in the sitting room and verandah. Gamal was keen on buying toys for his children. When he came home with a new toy, he would sit with them and teach them how to play with it. He was very loving with the children, talking and playing with them. When one of the babies grew up enough to sit at the table during meals, he would seat him next to him to teach him how to eat alone.

We had two cupboards in the dining room with a higher cupboard in the middle. One day Gamal came to me in the bedroom and handed me a key, telling me that there were grenades in the cupboard on the right and that he had locked it so that the children would not play with them. He asked me to keep the key safe. I hid the key, only getting it out when Gamal asked me for it, and found that I was afraid to go near the cupboard myself.

My visits to friends were very rare, and I didn't know any of the neighbors in our street. The lady who lived on the floor below me was old and she had daughters. Two of her daughters were nurses who spent most of their time at the hospital and I never saw them. The third daughter, who was married, came and visited me once with her daughter to play with Hoda and Mona. While we were seated in the living room, someone knocked at the door and asked for me, giving me a suitcase that was full of ammunition and bullets. I carried it into the bedroom as if it was empty and light, telling my guest that Gamal had sent the suitcase for me to pack his clothes because he had work out of Cairo the following day.

The atmosphere at home was secretive and worrying, but I did not understand the objective. I only knew I should be careful and reserved. One day I saw a book about one of the men close to the Prophet (PBUH), Abu Dhar al-Ghifari, the first socialist in Islam. Gamal came and saw me reading the book, and told me that the book was banned in Egypt and that he would return it in a couple of days. I became even more eager to read it and told myself that everything in the house was banned, even books!

My sisters' visits to me were rare. Whenever one of them came, we would sit in the living room, because Gamal had guests in the salon. My older sister once told me, "Whenever I come, you always have guests and the salon is occupied. The living room is cold." I told her that Gamal gave lessons to officers taking the staff officers examination.

We did not have a doorbell at our house and I often wondered why, but Gamal never explained and I never mentioned it.

I was happy and content with my life, and saw happiness around me and laughed a lot. Even though Gamal spent so many nights out of the house, it never occurred to me to be suspicious of him, and I was confident of his love and loyalty to me and his children. I was keen on making him happy and not to make any mistakes.

The officers who visited us and stayed for a short while, chatting and laughing loudly, were those I considered 'normal visitors,' whereas those who came at odd hours and were locked up with Gamal in the salon, speaking in hushed tones, I came to call 'the other ones' to myself.

Gamal was promoted to colonel and was assigned to a teaching position in the Staff Officers Academy. Since I first knew him, Gamal had been a teacher: first of students at the Military Academy; then of officers at the Administrative Affairs School; and now, finally, at the Staff Officers Academy. I had only ever seen Gamal teaching.

The new *murasil* was a poor, ignorant farmer. When he saw the guns, he would say that the colonel was "going into the desert with the officers to teach them."

When I got an unannounced visit from a friend, I would ask the *murasil* to move the guns into the study. Though leaving the lady waiting before admitting her into the house was not courteous, it was better than having her see the guns!

I was sitting in the living room one afternoon, after Gamal had gone out, when I saw the *murasil* carrying a large box filled with machine guns and going out the door. I asked him where he was going and he told me that "the colonel" had told him to clean the guns because he needed them for "teaching" the following day. He was going to clean them at the door to his room, which was close to the entrance of the building. I quickly thought of the danger of having people see the guns, so I told him that there would be many children playing around and that he might lose one of the pieces, which would be a big responsibility. The poor *murasil* got very worried and decided it would be safer to clean them in the kitchen.

THE GUNS ARE MOVED

Gamal told me that the guns I saw in the house were used against the British in cities like Suez. They wanted the British to feel unsafe, and he added that the plans for these operations were laid out in our house, and the men passing by him at all hours were collecting guns

ahia and Nasser: the wedding photograph, June 29, 1944

Tahia before marriage

Tahia's brother Abdel Hamid

Gamal Abdel Nasser (standing, center) with his father, uncle, and brothers

Nasser as a secondary
school student, 1931

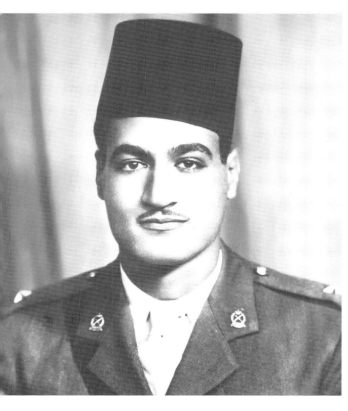

An early photograph
of Nasser at the Staff
Officers Academy, 1937

Colonel Gamal Abdel Nasser, at the time he proposed to Tahia

t al-Falluja in Palestine, 1948

Tahia en route to Yugoslavia, 11 July 1958

The picture of Tahia that Nasser kept on his desk, April 1961

Tahia on the island of Vanga, off Veliki Brijun, Yugoslavia, 1958

ahia votes in the elections of 1965

On the beach at Burg al-Arab

On a boat on the Nile, 1958

At Burg al-Arab, January 1960

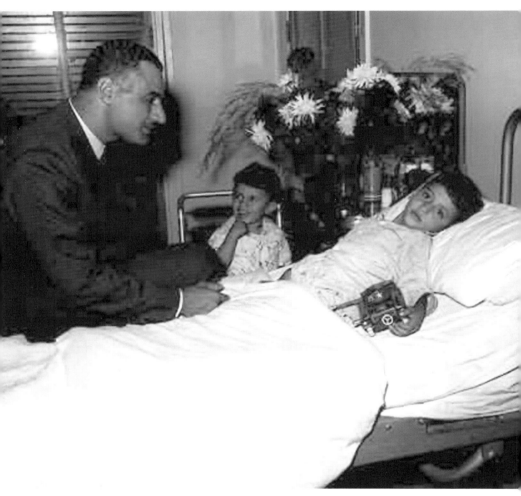

Visiting Khaled in hospital after his appendectomy, 3 November 1954

he President returns home after the Bandung Conference, to be greeted by his
hildren Hoda, Mona, Khaled, and Abdel Hamid, 2 May 1955

on their way to Suez. I asked him if he was going and he confirmed that he was, even though I pleaded with him not to.[5]

Another time, an officer brought a wrapped package in a bag for Gamal and left it with the *murasil*, telling him that the package contained two "folding beds" and that the colonel should choose the one he liked and return the other. The *murasil* actually believed him and repeated the message when Gamal got home. Gamal took the package into the bedroom and I followed him in, laughing at the poor man's naiveté, telling him that they were guns. Gamal said to me, "I know. It was I who sent them with the officer." This is what used to happen in our house, and yet I was always joyful, and happy and laughing.

THE TYPEWRITER AND MORE CAUTION WITH VISITORS

One day I found a typewriter placed on top of the cupboard that I never opened. After we finished our lunch, Gamal put the typewriter on the dining room table and started typing. I could hear the tapping of the keys and it was the first time I had seen Gamal using a typewriter. I told him, "I know you are working on something that you don't want to be written in your handwriting." He answered, "Don't worry yourself and think nothing of it." The typewriter remained in the dining room, on the cupboard, for days. I did not like how it looked in the room, so I placed it behind the cupboard where it could not be seen. When Gamal asked about it and I told him where I had put it, he did not object at all. I did not realize that having the typewriter in the house was dangerous; it was only that I did not like how it appeared in the room, and Gamal never said anything.

The typewriter remained with us for almost two years, and whenever Gamal used it, it was always at the same time, after lunch.

---

5 Before the Burning of Cairo in 1952, there were skirmishes between volunteer commandos *(fedayeen)* and the British in the Suez Canal Zone. Nasser, along with other Free Officers, used to train young officers there and provide them with provisions.

One day he told me to get rid of any papers in the house with names written on them. The small snippets of paper that had callers' names on them were placed either in the bedroom or on top of the piano. I was very careful not to lose any of Gamal's papers, but upon his instructions I burned them all.

I used to go out with Gamal to buy my clothes. We would agree on a time during a free afternoon and he would take me out to buy what I needed. I would try to choose my things as quickly as possible. Then I told him that it would be better for me to go alone in the morning and choose at my own leisure. Going alone in the morning was never very successful; using public transportation would invariably mean I was both late and tired when I got back, and I would find Gamal already home. So I told him that he was right and that I would go out with him to buy my things. Gamal used to laugh and answer, "Do as you wish."

Gamal was an organized man in all aspects. I was keen on having the house and the children always tidy and spruce. When we had guests, Hoda and Mona would often meet them before their father and sit with them in the salon. When Gamal joined them they would shake hands with the guests and politely leave the room. Even Khaled—when he learned to walk—would go into the salon and play with the guests until he was gently led out by his father, who would bring him to me, laughing, "I found him talking with the guests in the salon." As for myself, he always saw me well groomed and I was always careful to keep up an elegant appearance in the house.

1951

Hoda went to school at the Kubri al-Qubba School next to our house, where I could hear the school bell. I used to sit with her to help her learn how to write, filling pages with her attempts.

Hoda caught whooping cough, as did Mona and Khaled, and she was unable to go to school. We received letters from the school about her absence and we informed them that she was ill. Although she was better in a month, she was not allowed out of the house for two months, so Gamal told me to go and meet her teacher to be able to give Hoda her lessons at home so that she would not fall behind in her schoolwork. Hoda was a studious girl and we used to receive monthly reports applauding her efforts.

I went to the school at the end of the school day and met with Hoda's teacher. She told me that Hoda was one of her best students, and that she used to seat her at the front of the class, and she showed me Hoda's desk. When I explained the situation to her, she was kind enough to give me all the work that Hoda needed to do and to explain to me how to work with Hoda on her lessons. When I returned home, I told Gamal of my meeting with the teacher.

Before going out one morning, Gamal told me not to open the door to anyone before making sure I knew who it was, and even then to only open the top half of the door (the top half of the door had iron railings and glass that could be opened separately from the bottom half). I told him that I was doing that anyway these days, mainly because I had started my fourth pregnancy.

Another day, he told me that if anyone came to the house and asked to search it, I should be courageous and firmly refuse to admit anyone without my husband being there; that I should shut the door and not be afraid. I agreed very simply and without any worry or concern on my mind for I didn't have the time to be anxious.

Salah Salem used to come to our house at this time. Gamal often mentioned his name and told me that his children used to meet him when he went to visit him at the barracks in Abbasiya.

The months of my pregnancy were passing and the level of activity around me in the house was getting higher and higher. Gamal told me once, "I am very busy and preoccupied all the time." I told him, "I can see what is happening around me. I know it is unusual, and I know that it is all against the government, but to what end? What is the aim of all this?" He answered, "It is better that you don't know any details and stay as you are." I said, "Yes, I might make a mess if I ask too many questions." He laughed and said, "And ruin me." So I said, "Then it is better to leave me as I am: knowing nothing."

ABDEL HAMID'S BIRTH

Gamal was still teaching at the Staff Officers Academy during the last days of my pregnancy, coming with me to the regular check-ups. In the last week he told me to send him the *murasil* if I went into labor while he was at work and not to panic if he could not be found, telling me, "Be brave and take a taxi to the hospital till I come." He went out rarely during the evenings and would come home no later than ten.

While talking about the baby, I told him, "I would like another boy, so that Khaled is not spoiled by being the only brother of three sisters." But he told me, "Don't worry, I won't give him the chance to become spoiled."

My sister visited me one day and she suggested that I call the baby Abdel Hamid, after my brother. I mentioned this to Gamal and he approved, "We will call him Abdel Hamid." On 29 October 1951, Gamal went back to the academy in the evening and told me to send the *murasil* if I needed him. I started getting labor pains and sent for Gamal, who came quickly and took me to the hospital. Abdel Hamid was born at ten o'clock that night.

Gamal congratulated me, "Another boy. Are you happy?" And he said, "Abdel Hamid."

One afternoon in winter, when baby Mido was one month old, Gamal took me out shopping. We went to Fuad Street and Qasr al-Nil Street, and I bought what I needed, but the weather had changed, with heavy grey clouds in the sky. On our way home the rain started to beat down. No sooner had we arrived than Gamal got up and went out again. I was amazed that anyone would go out in such weather. When he came back at night, his shoes were wet. He told me that he had been out with Salah Salem and had driven him home in the car. When they approached the barracks they found that the whole area was flooded and they could not drive the car through the water, and Salah had to take off his shoes, roll up his trousers, and wade home. We laughed at the comic picture Gamal drew. His car managed to bring him home, but broke down before he reached the parking lot and he had to leave it in the street till morning. The next day, newspapers reported the heavy rains of the night before.

MORE VISITORS TO THE HOUSE

The number of visitors to the house increased, some of them coming before Gamal got home from work and sitting and waiting for him until he arrived, then talking with him for a few moments before leaving.

A visitor came and waited in the salon for Gamal to come home from work. When Gamal arrived, he asked me to prepare lunch for them. This same man came many times after that, at the same time. When the *murasil* opened the door and let him in, he would come to me and say, "It is the guest who waits for the colonel and has lunch." He never left a paper with his name on it, but Gamal told me that he was an officer who did not work in Cairo, but lived in al-Roda, near al-Minya, and was here on holiday. His name was Anwar al-Sadat.

Some months later, in the summer, a guest came in the early evening after Gamal had gone out. I opened the door to him myself and informed him that Gamal was not home. He left a paper with his name on it and I placed it on top of the piano. When Gamal returned, I told him that "a very dark officer" had called on him. He told me, "He is newly married, and his bride is very fair." It was Anwar al-Sadat.

The traffic of visitors to the house and Gamal's going out were increasing almost daily. One day, he suggested that we go to the cinema. I got myself and the children ready, prepared the baby's things, and sat in the living room listening to the radio until it was time to go. I waited and waited until the time of the film was long past, and still Gamal had not come out of the salon. When he finally emerged, he apologized, "I am sorry, I got very busy and the time passed. We will go another day." I got up and put my handbag back in the closet. I was not upset; all I felt was his love and appreciation.

He never forgot his children's birthdays and always bought them toys. I would wait till he came home so we could celebrate together, and I would make sure that the children stayed awake, even if he came back late.

JANUARY 1952

Hoda and Mona were at school, Khaled was two years old, and Abdel Hamid was two months. Although the activity in the house should have been worrying, I was too busy with my children and studying with Hoda and Mona to pay much attention to it. I remained Tahia, the happy and contented wife of beloved Gamal Abdel Nasser, the father of our beloved children, unconcerned by events around me. I carried out all my duties happily and felt peaceful in the evening, sitting in the living room or the study reading and listening to the radio, getting drowsy, and then going off to bed.

On 26 January, Gamal came home from work and told me about the fire, and I heard the details on the radio.[6] After lunch he got up to go out, so I said, "The fire is still burning." But he said, "Don't worry. I will go and see what is happening and come back." By nightfall he was still not back. I stood at the window of the study that overlooked the neighbor's garden. I could see the street, and the Qubba Palace, with the flag raised. I stood worrying and waiting in the cold. Why was he not back yet? When Gamal finally came home, he told me about what he had seen in the city, walking around the streets that had been ravaged by the fire.

The next day in the newspapers and on the radio they announced a curfew from 6pm; anyone walking on the streets would be shot.

---

6   On 25 January 1952, the British attacked an Egyptian police barracks on the Canal. The next day, in Cairo, crowds went out in demonstrations and set fire to establishments associated with the British presence, which became known as the Burning of Cairo or Black Saturday.

Gamal came home from work and after lunch went out in his regular clothes. Before six, I went out onto the verandah and looked down at the street. I could see Heliopolis Street and the Military Hospital Square; people were coming home on foot, alone or with families, and cars were driving past. The time was approaching six. I told myself, "Tonight he will be home early, and will stay at home, and we will not have any visitors," and I liked the thought.

Six o'clock came and went, and the streets were empty. Seven, eight, nine o'clock, and Gamal still had not come home. It was cold, and I had closed the windows of the verandah and stood on the inside watching the street and waiting for his car. By that time I was beside myself with worry; everyone had gone home and Gamal had still not come back.

At 10:30, Gamal came home. "I saw the light on in the salon," he said. "Who do you have with you?" "No one," I said, "I was waiting for you; I was very worried." My face reflected my concern. He laughed and tried to allay my fears. "I was at a friend's house, nearby in Zeitoun, and when I left I took the small side streets and didn't run into anyone."

The next day I read in the newspapers that army and police officers were allowed out during the curfew.

GAMAL ARMED AND IN UNIFORM

Things didn't change at our house, only the clothes. Gamal and his visitors all took to wearing their uniforms at all times.

One day an officer came to the house and asked to meet me. He handed me a dossier of files, which I opened. Papers were piled inside, all identical, and all critical of the government. I knew then they were anti-regime pamphlets and I quickly put them on top of the cupboard in the dining room (the one with the ammunition and grenades). For a moment, I was worried about having these pamphlets in the house. And I thought to myself, "That would be a catastrophe." But I soon forgot and busied myself in household affairs.

The following day, when I went into the dining room, the dossier was gone, and I was relieved. A few days later an open letter arrived, addressed to Colonel Gamal Abdel Nasser, which contained one of the pamphlets. I did not understand at all the reason for this or what was going on. I only feared for Gamal's safety if news should reach the prime minister or the king.

I was in the bedroom one evening with Gamal, who was getting dressed to go out. After putting on his shirt, he opened the closet and put on a shoulder holster with a gun, and then put on his jacket. "What are you wearing?" I asked in a state of shock. "Why are you carrying a gun?" I had broken down and started to cry. "Please don't worry yourself. I have enough troubles as it is. Would you prefer me to go out without the gun?" "No," I said, "do whatever you see fit." After he left I sat weeping in the sitting room, telling myself, "He can only be carrying a gun for two reasons: either he believes someone intends to shoot him; or he intends to shoot someone." Both cases, I felt, were disastrous. It was the first time I felt real fear and worry.

That night, he didn't stay out late. When he came back, I was lying on the bed, but not asleep. He greeted me as he always did and took off his clothes, placing his gun on top of the closet, with the bullets beside it. The following morning, he went to work as usual and when he came to go out at night I was not with him in the bedroom when he got dressed. After he left, I stood on a chair and looked on top of the closet to see if he had taken the gun. He had. After that it became normal practice for him to go out with the gun, always unloading it when he came home and placing it and the bullets on top of the closet, near the edge for easy reach. With time, I started to get used to the idea and would even bring him the gun myself before he went out.

One day, while I was bringing him the gun, he called out, "Be careful, I didn't unload it last night!" I got into the habit of thanking God on the nights he went out without a gun, believing that it meant he was in a safe place, and lying awake on the nights he took the gun with him, only sleeping when I heard him come in, unload the bullets, and place the gun on top of the closet.

At times I would fall asleep and wake up to the sound and lights of the car in the road. I would hear him walking from the parking lot and climbing the stairs. At times, I would watch him from the window, or go out and meet him in the sitting room, or sometimes open the door for him, keeping the lights off, and he would laughingly greet me.

One day Gamal was taking me and the children to visit my sister in Giza, as he did when he was going out somewhere near there. After welcoming us, my sister asked about Gamal, "We haven't seen him for a long time. Why doesn't he come upstairs with you and sit with us for a while?" I remembered the gun then and thought that my sister had no idea what was happening with Gamal.

I read in the newspapers about an officer who had been shot while walking home in al-Roda. I feared for Gamal's safety from the king and the government, but I never mentioned anything to him. When he went out without his gun, I started asking him if I should get it for him, and he would tell me he was only going out near the house and didn't need it. He would laugh that it was I who was reminding him.

Gamal used to sit and type after lunch, then send what he had written with the *murasil*. I used to hear him repeat Gamal's instructions to him, "I will take the papers to Abeid Effendi at Kubri al-Qubba Station on the first floor." On his return I would hear him tell Gamal that he had taken the papers to Abeid Effendi. But Abeid Effendi had never visited our house. Only after the Revolution, when I read about Hamdi Abeid being assigned the post of minister of state, did I realize that he was Abeid Effendi. The printing press for the pamphlets was at his house in Kubri al-Qubba.

Khaled Mohieddin used to visit us and I remember Gamal telling me the story of his young daughter's illness; she was only a few months old and Gamal was very sad about it.

Prelude to the Revolution

THE START OF SUMMER 1952

Our household remained the same: visitors at all hours both before and after the Ramadan *iftar*, and late nights out of the house. When Ramadan ended and we celebrated the feast, Gamal suggested we go and visit my sisters in Giza, who both lived in the same building. We took the car with Hoda, Mona, Khaled, and Mido.

When we were close to the house, Gamal asked me if I would like him to drive us up to the Pyramids since the weather was agreeable; I agreed and thanked him, thinking it would be nice for the children.

While we were driving along, we came to a mailbox. Gamal stopped the car and reached for a large envelope. This large envelope contained many smaller envelopes that he deposited in the mailbox. After doing this we continued on our drive and went on to my sisters' house. I realized, of course, that those were pamphlets, but I mentioned nothing to Gamal.

Right after the feast, Gamal told me that he had two weeks' holiday before starting exams at the academy, and he suggested we take the children to Alexandria for ten days. I agreed to the idea; I had not been to Alexandria since our marriage eight years earlier. Gamal went sometimes for short visits, maybe a day or two, to see his father and brothers. It was 29 June 1952.

On our wedding anniversary, we traveled with the children to Alexandria in our black Austin. Gamal mentioned that it was a strange coincidence to be going with our children to Alexandria exactly eight years after going as newlyweds. He had already booked a hotel for us—a newly built one in Sidi Bishr. He told me that he planned to spend the morning with us at the beach, swimming with the children. He would then go out for a short while, come back, and take us out in the evening. Then, at night, he would go out and meet his officer friends. I asked him if "they" had followed us all the way to Alexandria, and he laughed and said that yes, "they" were there, but some had remained in Cairo.

Most of the government officials at the time had houses in Sidi Bishr. I would hear Gamal talking about Hussein Sirri, saying that he had traveled or that he had come back. When we passed in front of his house, which was near our hotel, he would mention his name. I did not give the matter much attention, thinking nothing of it at the time.

We would go to the beach in the morning and Gamal would take Hoda, Mona, and Khaled swimming while I sat in the shade with baby Mido in his stroller. He was only eight months old. We would go back to the hotel for lunch and then Gamal would go out in the afternoon. When he returned, he would tell me that he had been sitting in a nearby casino with his officer friends. We would then take the car and go out, parking to take a stroll and watch the sunset. He would take us back to the hotel for supper and then he would go out. The children would sleep and I would sit on the verandah.

On 10 July, we returned from Alexandria to Cairo. Gamal had decided to take the agricultural road. Along the way, I read signs that showed land owned by members of the royal family and rich landowners. "All this land is owned by princes and pashas?" I asked him. He said, "Not for long. There will soon be no land owned by princes or pashas!" I did not really pay attention to his reply, and did not comment or understand much.

A few days after our return from Alexandria, his brothers came to visit us. Our house seemed to be in a frenzy of activity, people coming and going at all hours. Gamal would come home from work and there would be someone waiting for him daily. He would ask for lunch and then they would go out, not coming back before dawn. It was summer and it was hot. I used to wake up several times during the night, waiting for his return, going to look out of the window. He continued to go out with the gun.

THE LAST WEEK BEFORE THE REVOLUTION

When Gamal came home just before dawn one night, I told him, "I am afraid for you and our children." He said, "All you are concerned about in your country is your husband and children, your own family, alone? That is very selfish . . . don't you care for your country?" As he made his way to the door, he turned and said, "Come, let us sit together with my brothers in the sitting room. They have woken up." His brothers used to put a makeshift bed in the study at night for sleeping. I sat with them awhile, then rose to leave them. "Where are you going?" he said. "I am going to pray." He said, "Quickly then, before the sun rises." And he looked at me with love and tenderness.

I had no understanding of the means or the end of what was happening. I only understood the danger of what was happening before me.

A few days before the Revolution, he told me that he was very busy at the academy; it was exam time and he had papers to correct. He told me to go out with my sisters, to maybe take Hoda, Mona, and Khaled to the cinema. There were a few cinemas in Heliopolis, mostly summer cinemas, and the weather was hot and one was also within walking distance. I liked the idea, and took the children and went to the cinema.

In the morning he told me to make extra food at lunch for some officers coming to visit him. People came and went, and he went out himself, either with them or alone. He worked most of the time and hardly slept. The two nights before the Revolution he did not sleep, sitting and working at the dining-room table, then coming into the bedroom at seven in the morning and changing into his uniform, having breakfast, and leaving. He would tell me, "Make extra food, we are going to work late like last night, correcting papers."

Abdel Hamid was eight months old, and seemed poorly. I needed to take him to the doctor for a check-up and change of feeding schedule. When Gamal came home from work he went in to play with him and found him unwell. I told him, "We need to take him to the doctor, when are you free to take us?" "I am very busy," he said. "Ask the doctor to come to the house or take him by taxi." This was the first time ever he had not found the time to take one of his children to the doctor, and the next day I took Abdel Hamid alone.

The 23 July Revolution

THE EVE OF THE REVOLUTION

It was 22 July 1952. At seven o'clock, Gamal, who had been up all night working in the dining room, came in and greeted me before getting dressed in his uniform and having breakfast with me.

He came back in the afternoon and had lunch with the officers. They sat together in the salon and then they left. He asked me, "Why don't you go with my brothers to the cinema and take Hoda, Mona, and Khaled? The weather is hot; it would be nice to go out." I agreed to go.

He went out before us, and, at sunset, I decided I would prefer to take a walk by the gardens. The streets were not as crowded then as they are today; they were lined with villas and shaded with trees, and I enjoyed the fragrance of the flowers from the gardens.

I went out for my walk with Hoda, Mona, and Khaled, and was back before eight o'clock. His brother told me that Gamal had come home and asked about me and the children, and they had told him I had gone out for a walk. Some time later, he came home dressed in trousers and a shirt, and asked me why I had changed my mind and not gone to the cinema. I told him, "I thought it better to have a walk in the open air and not to leave Abdel Hamid alone for too long." He kissed the children and played with them, calling them by the names of endearment he used for them, and with Abdel Hamid, whom I was carrying on my shoulder. He then went out again.

The children had their supper and slept early as usual. Abdel Hamid had his nine o'clock feed and also slept, and I sat with Leithi and Shawqi, Gamal's brothers.

Before eleven, he came into the bedroom as I was lying in bed. He washed his face and I thought, "He always washes his face before sleeping; he has not slept for two nights and it seems tonight he will sleep early." But, to my surprise, he opened the closet and took out his uniform and started getting dressed. I could not help myself from saying, "Where are you going in your uniform at this hour?" It was the first time since our marriage that I had asked him where he was going. He very calmly replied, "I must finish correcting papers for the academy. The last two nights I worked here at home and my colleague suggested that tonight we work at his house. I might not be back tonight and will go straight to work in the morning. I will see you for lunch." He then said goodbye and walked out of the room, telling me not to go into the sitting room because there was an officer waiting for him outside.

When I heard the front door close, I got up and went into the study where his brothers were sitting. "Gamal has been detained," I said. His brother Leithi replied, "Don't worry, Gamal is fine." I thought he had been detained because I remembered when it had happened before; an officer had waited for him and he had worn his uniform when Ibrahim Abdel Hadi ordered his arrest.

I could see what was happening: the frenzy in the house since our return from Alexandria; the constant visits; and the late nights out. I was sure that the newly appointed prime minister, Naguib al-Hilali, had detained him. His brother kept urging me not to worry, until he finally swore on the Holy Qur'an that Gamal had not been detained. We sat together in the study, his brothers and I, and I got up and prepared a light supper for us. At midnight, I got up to sleep, only to hear gunshots a few moments later. The shots were coming from the direction of the

Qubba Palace. I ran out of the room and found his brothers in the sitting room. "Those shots . . . they are from the palace! Gamal is surely one of those attacking the palace!" And I cried. The shots continued for around ten minutes, and then there was silence . . . and then the shots started again, and I was in tears, so Gamal's brother told me it was known that the sound of shots comes from the opposite direction, not from where they are fired, so they were not from the palace. His eye went to the Qur'an, but I stopped him, saying, "Don't swear again about anything you do not know for sure. I will not believe you."

After a while, I felt his brothers might want to go to sleep and so I left them and went into my bedroom. When the house grew silent outside, I crept out and looked out through the window of the dining room at the street. While I was standing in the dark, I noticed his two brothers on the verandah. When they saw me, they said, "We were waiting for you to sleep to see what was happening outside." I said, "Me too. I also waited for you to sleep to investigate." I asked them to go inside because I was sure our house was under surveillance by the police and the authorities.

I stayed awake, going from the window to the verandah, where I could see the street clearly, trying to keep out of sight.

At around one in the morning I saw a young man standing at the corner by the Military Hospital Square.

The young man, who was tall and well-built, was calling out to the cars passing by and blocking their entry into the street, forcing them to turn around and take side streets. I did not realize that the confident, sure-footed young man shouting out in the dead of night was Colonel Gamal Abdel Nasser, my beloved husband.

I stood there watching the young man and wondering what had happened during the gun fight, my only concern being that Gamal was not harmed.

Shortly before two, I saw armored cars, tanks, and the army, which had been provided with arms after the war in Palestine. I saw and heard them on the streets, moving toward the Military Hospital

hia with Abdel Hakim, 1958

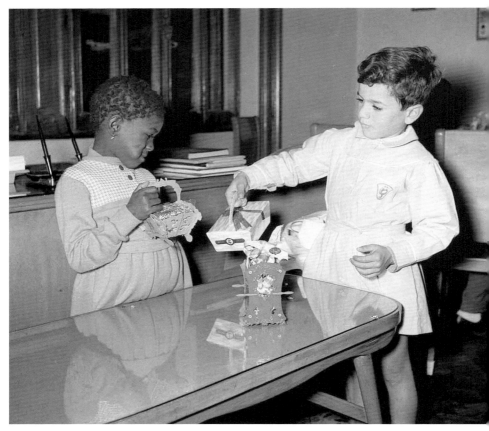

Abdel Hakim Abdel Nasser plays with Juliana, daughter of Patrice Lumumba, prime minister of the Republic of the Congo, 10 November 1960

With Hoda, Mona, Khaled, and Abdel Hamid

Celebrating Abdel Hamid's birthday, 29 October 1958

eeting Soviet cosmonaut Yuri Gagarin, January 1962

The family in the garden at Manshiyat al-Bakri 30 March 1963

haled, Abdel Hamid, and Abdel Hakim Abdel Nasser with the children of Patrice
umumba, 10 November 1960

عيد سعيد يا ماما

Abdel Hakim wishes his mother a Happy Mother's Day

The family at home in Manshiyat al-Bakri, 1 January 1960

The family at home in Manshiyat al-Bakri, 1965

The family welcomes President Walter Ulbricht of East Germany at Manshiyat al-Bakri,
4 February 1965

Nasser walks with his sons in the garden at Manshiyat al-Bakri, 1965

The President introduces his family to Sirimavo Bandaranaike, prime minister of Ceylon, at Manshiyat al-Bakri, 10 October 1963

Tahia with Abdel Hamid, Manshiyat al-Bakri

Khaled, Abdel Hakim, and Abdel Hamid in Tsqaltubo, Georgia, 1968

Tahia walks with Abdel Hamid in the garden of Manshiyat al-Bakri, on his first visit home from the Naval Academy

Tahia with her daughter Hoda and grandchildren, 1968

Tahia with Hoda, Abdel Hamid, and his wife at their wedding, Alexandria, 16 August 1973

ahia and Nasser with eldest daughter Hoda at the Nile Barrages

asser and Tahia with their daughters and sons-in-law, Manshiyat al-Bakri

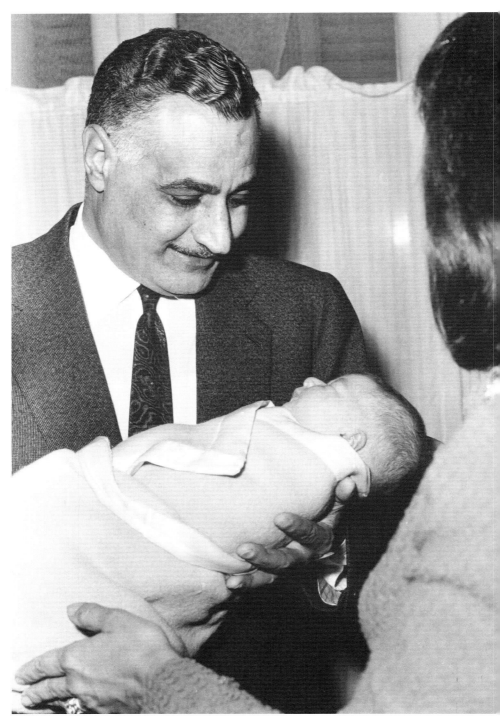

Nasser holds his first grandchild Hala, soon after her birth

Square. I knew the location of the army barracks close to our house, which I had seen when I took walks.

At that moment his brothers jumped up in joy and embraced each other, and shouted, "Be happy, be happy!" I said, "But where is Gamal? What about the gunshots?" And then, in the midst of my tears, I understood that it was a military coup.

His brothers congratulated me, but I kept on crying, "If only I knew where Gamal was and about the gunshots we heard." His brother told me, "Gamal told us on his way out that he had a dangerous mission; if we saw the army on the streets we would know that he had succeeded and that he was fine. If nothing happened then we should search for him in the morning." Once more I said, "I understand now that it is a military coup and that it has succeeded, but where is Gamal? I just want to know that he is safe." I sat until morning, unable to go into the bedroom.

CONGRATULATIONS

At 6:30 on the morning of 23 July 1952, there was a knock on the door. When Gamal's brother answered, he found Tharwat Okasha standing there, asking to meet me. He shook my hand and congratulated me. "The military coup has succeeded." I asked him about Gamal. He told me, "He is close by, not more than five minutes away at the General Command. Do you know where that is?" I said, "Of course I know; I walk past it often." He told me to listen to the statement on the radio at seven o'clock. I thanked him and he left.

We switched on the radio and waited for the statement that was finally aired at 7:20. It was read by Anwar al-Sadat.

At 9:30 an officer called, saying he had come from the General Command at Kubri al-Qubba and that he was sent by Colonel Gamal Abdel Nasser to tell me that he was fine and would not be home for lunch, and that he was at the General Command.

My brother Mustafa came while I was in the sitting room with Gamal's brothers. After we shook hands, I asked him to sit down, but he said, "I am in a hurry. I left my office and came. I have people waiting for me. I told them I would not be long. I have no time to sit down." In an agitated voice, he continued, "I have seen the streets, the army and tanks are everywhere. They have surrounded the radio building and all the important squares and streets in the city. I heard there was a military coup, and I was worried about Colonel Gamal and came to see him. I hope he is not one of the officers involved; the king will not leave them, he will hang them all, I am sure of it." I answered, "Gamal is not involved in politics." He asked, "What time did he leave this morning?" I said, "At the usual hour, before eight." And he left before I could offer him a coffee or juice.

I caught the look in the eyes of Gamal's brothers and we smiled. When we heard my brother's car drive away, we could not contain our laughter. I was not concerned in the least by my brother's words, which to me were nonsense and made me laugh.

We spent the day listening to the radio and the reading of the statement. We could hear the airplanes flying overhead toward Kubri al-Qubba and around Cairo. At ten in the evening, Gamal returned home. I congratulated him with all my heart. He told me he could stay for two hours before going back.

He shaved and bathed, changed his clothes, and came to sit with us. I told him about my brother's visit that morning and what he had said—omitting the part about the king and his expected actions—and my answers. He said that my brother was in for a big surprise the next morning when he read the newspapers and saw pictures of Gamal in a jeep with General Mohamed Naguib—it was the first time I heard the name—when they had toured Cairo and all the country had taken to the streets to cheer them fervently.

I told him that I had been hearing the planes overhead all day, and I told him how worried I had been about him, how I had waited for him all night, and my fears after hearing the gunshots.

Gamal said, "We attacked the General Command with an army battalion, and I had Abdel Hakim Amer with me. Only two soldiers were hurt, one from each side. All the officers present were in a meeting at the time and they surrendered. I took them one by one to the Military Secondary School in Manshiyat al-Bakri." He continued, "I handed them over to Hamdi Ashour, the prison guard, and then I went and stood at the corner at the Military Hospital to divert the cars and had the Austin parked close by." He started to laugh, "How could you be so worried when I was standing at the corner, so close, with our car parked next to me?" I said, "You were so close, yet so far away." And he continued to laugh.

He spoke of the king, saying that he had sent them an emissary. They had stated their demands and conditions, and the king had agreed to them immediately.

I told him that Tharwat Okasha had come in the morning to congratulate me and tell me to listen to the statement on the radio. He told me, "That was Anwar al-Sadat. He was with his wife at the cinema, and when he got home he found a paper waiting for him telling him to come to us. He dressed in his uniform and quickly left the house. When he approached Heliopolis, the officer posted there refused to let him through because he didn't know the password. After arguing and cajoling him, he managed to pass only to be stopped again at the General Command building, so he drove around to the back, but to no avail. Then, finally, he shouted out and Abdel Hakim heard him and let him in at dawn. I then gave him the statement to read. "

Gamal was laughing as he told us the story of Anwar al-Sadat.

At midnight, he rose to leave, telling me not to wait for him because he would be staying at the General Command. He said goodbye and left.

THE FIRST DAYS

On 24 July 1952, all the morning newspapers wrote about the army and the coup.

I saw pictures of Gamal Abdel Nasser and of Abdel Hakim Amer, his friend, and of Salah Salem, who came to our house often and whose name Gamal mentioned, and Kamal al-Din Hussein (who also came to our house, although Gamal only ever referred to him as Kamal without his surname), Gamal Salem (who also came but whom I never personally knew), Abdel Latif Baghdadi (whom I had not seen, and whose name I did not remember hearing or reading on one of the snippets of paper), Zakaria Mohieddin (the study partner from the Academy days), Khaled Mohieddin (who had given me the pamphlets), Hassan Ibrahim, and Anwar al-Sadat, the dark visitor. There was also a picture of Gamal with General Mohamed Naguib, whom I had never heard of at all. Later, I heard the name of Hussein al-Shafei as one of the members of the Revolutionary Command Council.

Gamal remained at the General Command Center until 26 July, when he came home at five in the morning. He told me that the king was to leave Egypt on board *al-Mahrousa* at six that night. Gamal Salem had traveled to Alexandria to set up the departure of the king, and the army had surrounded all the palaces of the royal family in Cairo and Alexandria. He told me to listen to the news at six o'clock. He sat and talked with us for an hour, and then said his goodbyes and went back to the command center.

After the evening of the Revolution, we had two soldiers posted at the door to our building and two at the end of the street. They would ask any passers-by where they were going, and if anyone came to our building one of the soldiers would come upstairs with them. If they were going to a neighbor, the soldier would leave, but if they were coming to our apartment, the soldier would remain standing until we opened the door and admitted the caller.

Gamal gave orders to the *murasil* to take care of the soldiers, offering them tea, coffee, and water. He also told us to prepare lunch and supper for them, which we did. Gamal rarely came home and slept at the house. When he did, he would leave very early in the morning and he hardly saw the children, only for a few moments before leaving.

The *murasala* system was ended in the first week after the Revolution, but the man assigned to our house refused to leave. "Where will I go?" he said. "What would I do back in the village? My family is very poor. I will remain with Colonel Gamal." And so he was allowed to stay and was given a different salary until a suitable position could be found for him, which happened when he was assigned to the presidential security. As for our first *murasil*, who was with Gamal during the Palestine War, Gamal saw him once in a crowd during a visit to Upper Egypt. The man waved his hand, trying to get close to Gamal, who called him over and learned that he was going through hard times, and so he was assigned to security at Manshiyat al-Bakri.

Gamal told me that I could not go out alone. The car was in the parking lot and he would send me an army driver if I needed to go out with the children. I went and visited my sisters and the wife of Abdel Hakim Amer, and saw the tanks at the entrance to Heliopolis.

We hardly saw Gamal at the house; only on some days when he had slept at home would we see him for breakfast. Before going out on those days, he would receive officers at the house who came with requests or complaints of injustices for him to resolve. He spent days on end at the General Command and took what clothes he needed and his shaving kit with him there. He used to send a soldier in a jeep to pick up anything he needed from the house.

We had a telephone installed in the house. I didn't really pay much heed to it, having never felt I lacked it in the first place. My first telephone conversation was with a relative of the doctor I visited during my pregnancies, calling with a request. I was surprised that she knew me or knew my name, then I remembered that the doctor knew my name. She told me that her brother had told her I had given birth to two sons at his hospital. I received visits from wives of prominent army personnel, asking for favors for their husbands, some of whom had been discharged from the army during the 'cleansing' process following the Revolution. Other non-military wives visited with requests and stories of injustice from the times of the king, wanting solutions to their problems. All the letters of complaints and requests left by the ladies I would hand over to Gamal.

Some of them complained about the injustices of the *waqf* system that did not give women their fair share of an inheritance compared to their brother or father. They also complained about living in poverty while their brothers lived in luxury and wealth. I listened with interest to all these stories.

The wall at the end of the road, beside the lot where we parked our Austin, was knocked down and the road was now open at both ends.

THE FIRST ISSUE OF *AL-GUMHURIYA* NEWSPAPER

A few months after the Revolution, Gamal became involved in publishing a new daily newspaper. He worked late into the night on the details of the new publication, discussing them over the phone and working on the drafts that I saw around the house, until finally *al-Gumhuriya* ('The Republic') was issued.

I remember how happy he looked when he handed me the first issue. I have always held the paper in high regard because I know how much it meant to Gamal.

There were many important articles published in the paper under the name of Anwar al-Sadat, but they were written by Gamal Abdel Nasser. After reading one of these articles I told him that I recognized his words and his style, and I asked him, "Did you write this?" And he answered, "Yes."

MOVING TO THE HOUSE IN MANSHIYAT AL-BAKRI, OCTOBER 1952

Gamal told me that we needed to move because we could no longer live in a house with neighbors, and there were two houses available for us: a big house with two floors and ten rooms at the barracks in Abbasiya or another smaller house with five rooms in Manshiyat al-Bakri. I asked him if the smaller house was close to the Heliopolis Road, and he said that it was. I told him I would prefer the house on the main road and not in the barracks in Abbasiya. He told me to go ahead and choose the one I wanted, and that I needed to organize the move because he was busy. I could send the *murasil* with vans to move the furniture, and, once we had moved and were ready, I should let him know. I did as Gamal instructed, and on 20 October 1952, we moved into our new house. Like our other two houses, when I walked into it, it was the first time I had seen it.

At one in the afternoon I was in our black Austin being driven with the children, Hoda, Mona, Khaled, and Abdel Hamid, to the new house in Manshiyat al-Bakri. When we arrived, I found a number of soldiers at the door and soldiers in the garden. In front of the house were two cannons and some military police, and there were two cannons on the roof of the house as well. The house was surrounded by a very large garden and a high wall. There was a small white stone structure built beside the wall to the right of the main entrance. It did not look residential at all, but built more as a military barracks or offices, surrounded by a large garden without flowers or shrubs, except for some ancient eucalyptus trees. The house had the usual three doors, the middle one leading straight through a central corridor to a back door to the garden. The door to the right opened onto the bedroom, and the one on the left onto the salon. The three doors were accessed by a verandah that was elevated by one step from the garden and had a small wooden fence painted green. On the left of the central corridor was the dining room that led into the salon, to the right were a bedroom and study, at the back of which was a smaller area with a window to the garden, where I placed Abdel Hamid's bed. Off a small corridor there was a large bedroom for the children.

I looked around me at the house that did not look like a home at all—full of corridors and rooms leading onto rooms, a dry, patchy garden, cannons and soldiers—and I missed my sitting room and my verandah overlooking the street and the Military Hospital Square, and I even missed the people walking in the street.

I asked, "Why all of this? Why the soldiers and the cannons?" I was told that the commander of the military police had been there in the morning and had arranged everything. His name was Ahmed Anwar, and I remembered having read his name on one of the slips of paper left at our house, but I did not know him. I remained silent.

At night the garden was full of strong lights and I could not sleep. It was around one o'clock, while I was lying on the bed, that I heard Gamal's car come through the gate to the house. I heard him call out, "What's this? Put out these lights. Send the soldiers away, only a couple at the gate and a couple of military police are enough. Remove the cannons and the guns!" The soldier on duty said he would sleep in the guard house by the gate, and Gamal later told us to make supper for him.

Gamal came into the bedroom and greeted me, surprised that I was still awake, and asked me if I liked the house. I told him that I did not. He said, "You will get used to it. When the garden is planted it will look much better, and I asked the security personnel to leave. What was Ahmed Anwar thinking of?" I told him that I had thought I would have to try to sleep with the floodlights on and that now the lights were off I would be able to get some sleep, and that I had heard him give his orders.

We organized the house and got the garden in order and planted flowers, and I started getting used to living there, with the military atmosphere around me. I got used to hearing the bugle call from the barracks and the footsteps of marching soldiers.

On 29 October 1952, Abdel Hamid turned one. We had been at the house for nine days. Gamal came home, and had lunch with us and played with the children. Picking up Abdel Hamid and kissing him, he told me that I would have to celebrate the birthday alone because he needed to leave. I had invited my sisters.

On the day after his birthday, Abdel Hamid fell ill and I called the children's doctor to come to the house. When he came to leave, the doctor refused to take any money. "Do you know how much money I made today? It is the least I can offer to Colonel Gamal Abdel Nasser, to take care of his children, and don't even tell him the boy is ill; he has too much to worry about. I will call tomorrow morning to check up on him and pass by in the evening." I appreciated the attitude of the doctor, Dr. Mustafa al-Diwani, and his noble gesture, remembering the times I would wait for hours at his clinic. It was the first of many noble gestures I received.

The Revolutionary Council used to meet at the Command Center at Kubri al-Qubba, or at a building in Qasr al-Nil, or at the Council headquarters in Gezira, in a new building that had been built by King Farouk.

Gamal sometimes came home in the early morning, around seven, and he would knock on the bedroom door and we would laugh as we greeted each other with a "Good morning." He would then sleep and wake up again at around eleven to go back to his meetings. I would leave him to get his much needed rest, and go and wake Hoda and Mona for school.

The Council sometimes used to meet at our house. They would stay up all night until morning, sometimes till the afternoon, before dispersing, then coming back and continuing at night for days on end.

I never saw General Mohamed Naguib taking part in the meetings at our house. The laws that were announced, and that I read about in the newspapers and heard about on the radio, came after these meetings at the house. I would often hear Gamal, before going out, calling to one of the officers and giving him an envelope, asking him to go to General Naguib to get his signature on a new official decree and bring it back quickly to Gamal at the Council or the Command Center.

We now had a telephone in the study and two telephones in the bedroom, one on the nightstand and one by the bed. Before Gamal came home in the evenings, I would receive abundant telephone calls at all hours asking for Gamal and asking when he would be available at home. This might have been a normal question for the caller, but it was not a normal question for me. I was awoken often by calls during the night and I would answer and take messages. I received calls from ministers, which was very strange to me: a minister before had always been "Your Excellency," and there had never been any cause for any minister to call our house, but now it was a regular occurrence. I got calls from the wives of former pashas and I even received a call one morning from the mother of the former Queen Nariman asking for Gamal Abdel Nasser.

I remember once that the minister of religious endowments called him, and the man pronounced his ministry using Classical Arabic (*awqaf*) and not the Egyptian colloquial pronunciation (*aw'af*). When Gamal came home, I was sleeping and I groggily raised my head and told him that the minister had called, repeating his Classical Arabic pronunciation wrongly as *qawqaf*. Gamal laughed and it became our private joke with any cabinet change for me to ask about the "minister of *qawqaf*."

There were many calls from journalists wanting to know when he would be heading from the Council or the Command Center to the house, as well as many officers, some of whose names I remembered from the snippets of paper. All these messages would be relayed to Gamal when he came home, when he would sit and return the calls.

He would make his calls, give his orders and instructions, and call the editors-in-chief of the newspapers, and I remained silent by his side, sometimes listening and sometimes falling asleep. This could last till one, two, or three in the morning if he had come home in the evening. On the days he came back at seven in the morning, he would sleep and go back out at noon.

This was how we lived after moving to the house in Manshiyat al-Bakri.

Umm Kulthum called me one day and said that she had met Colonel Gamal Abdel Nasser the previous night at the Command

Center, and she had asked him about me and wanted to visit me. I gave her an appointment. Umm Kulthum's telephone call was the one that pleased me most, and she was the guest I welcomed and received with the most pleasure at our house.

The Declaration of the Republic

A SLIGHT PAIN, MAY 1953

Gamal had an abdominal pain that I did not know of for some time because he was out of the house most of the day.

One day, before going out, he told me that he would be back for lunch and asked me to prepare a light meal of boiled vegetables because he had a slight pain in his stomach. I made the lunch and waited for him, but he did not show up. I thought nothing of it, believing that he had been delayed and had not had the time to come home. Later, I received a visit from Abdel Hakim Amer, who asked to see me. He said, "Gamal is fine. He has regained consciousness after the anesthetic. He had his appendix taken out. He is asking to see you at the hospital."

I was shocked. "How could he have an operation without telling me? He asked me to prepare a light lunch!" "I was with him and he is fine," said Abdel Hakim.

I went to the Mazhar Ashour Hospital to see Gamal. "How could you not tell me?" I asked. "I didn't want to worry you. I had planned for the operation the day before and came to the hospital this morning with Abdel Hakim, and told you to make me lunch so that you wouldn't know about it." And he smiled and said, "I'm fine."

I used to go and visit him every day and take the children with me, because he asked to see them. I did not stay long on each visit because he had so many visitors. I met Abdel Latif Baghdadi and his wife, whom I had not met before, and she said that she would visit me.

A week later, Gamal came home, and a few days after that we went to Marsa Matruh with the children for his convalescence. Dr. Mazhar Ashour accompanied us to be close to Gamal, and we invited his wife and daughter to join us.

We stayed at a very old house in Matruh, very simply furnished with only the bare necessities; it did not even have a dining table, just some chairs and a table in the sitting area. Gamal Salem came and stayed with us for the duration, and we returned to Cairo after a week.

The requests and complaints kept pouring in. People would send letters by post or leave messages with the officers to hand to Gamal. He asked me not to meet any of the ladies whom he did not know until I had asked him first.

I fell on my leg and had to have it in plaster for two weeks. When I went to Mazhar Ashour Hospital to have the plaster removed and physiotherapy on my leg, I was told that Anwar al-Sadat's wife was there after having an operation on her finger. I went to visit her, and that was the first time we met.

MOHAMED NAGUIB AT OUR HOUSE

I woke up to the sound of cars coming through the gates to our house. I got up and looked out of the window and saw all the members of the Revolutionary Council, as well as General Mohamed Naguib. I had heard about the declaration of the Republic[7] and I said to myself, "I was asleep and woke up in the middle of the night to find the president in my house!" They spent a short time and when they left, Gamal came into the room and found me standing. He told me about General Naguib's insistence that he pay a visit to Gamal at home after the declaration of the Republic.

---

7   The Republic was declared on 18 June 1953, after the King's removal on July 26, 1952 and abdication of his throne in favor of his son Ahmed Fuad, and the formation of the Regency Council under Prince Mohamed Abdel Moneim.

Conspiracies

THE CAVALRY CONSPIRACY,
MAY 1954

Gamal came home before sunset and told me to pack a bag and take the children to my sister's, and stay the night there. He told me I had to leave before eight because he was expecting an attack on the house, even an attempt to destroy it with cannon fire. I was to stay at my sister's until he called me to come back.

I packed my bags and called for the black Austin, which I used for going out, to wait for me in the garden. Gamal was in the salon with some officers and I sat in the study, waiting for him to finish. At eight o'clock he came out of the salon and saw me and the children sitting there. He became very agitated and asked why I had not left the house. I told him I was waiting for him to come out and tell me to go. He said, "I must go to the Command Center now. How can I leave while you are still in the house?" "I am ready to go and the car is waiting outside," I said. We left the house at the same time, each of us taking a separate car.

I went to my sister's house, arriving after nine. She was surprised as she let us in, saying, "It's late. Where have you been with the children?" I told her why we were there and saw the look of worry on her face and her husband's.

I spent a worried, restless night, wondering what had happened at the house. In the morning, as my sister and I were having breakfast with the children, the telephone rang. It was Gamal Abdel Nasser.

He told me that I could go back to the house. He had sent me the car and he was going to sleep. I took leave of my sister, who wanted us to stay for lunch, and made my way back to the house. Gamal was still awake when I arrived. He told me that it had been a conspiracy by the cavalry. They had had all the information about the conspiracy and were ready to move against them and apprehend the officers involved. But he had been worried about any mishap in timing. What if a tank had made its way to the house? And so he had thought it better to be on the safe side and have the house empty. I thanked God for our safety.

THE ASSASSINATION ATTEMPT AT AL-MANSHIYA

In the summer of 1954, we traveled to Alexandria, where we had rented the first floor of a villa on the Corniche. We were sharing the villa, as another family had rented the second floor.

Gamal used to come every week or two and spend a day with us, and then head back to Cairo, to the house in Manshiyat al-Bakri. In August he went on the pilgrimage to Mecca. I traveled to Cairo to welcome him home on his return and stayed for a few days before going back to Alexandria, where I stayed until September.

At the end of October, Gamal was scheduled to give a speech in Alexandria at al-Manshiya Square. He left the house in the early evening. It was his habit to put a small Qur'an contained in a white metal box in his pocket. He searched everywhere for it and so did I—in a great hurry since he was running late—but we could not find it. And so I gave Gamal another one with a cardboard cover. When he was at the door, I suddenly found his original Qur'an and raced to catch up with him and give it to him. He took it and placed it in his pocket, going out with two. The assassination attempt—eight bullets fired at him—happened while he was giving his speech at al-Manshiya, and he survived.[8] Ever after that, Gamal continued to go out of the house with two Holy Books, until the day he died. He would come back home and put them side by side in the same place in the bedroom. They are very dear to me and I have kept them ever since.

Gamal called me after the assassination attempt. He told me I would hear the news on the radio, and that he was fine and I was not to worry.

A couple of days later, Khaled, aged four years and eight months, got appendicitis. I called Dr. Mazhar Ashour to come and see him and he told us that Khaled would have to have an immediate operation. Gamal was going out to a meeting and he came to see the doctor before he went. He told him to take whatever measures were necessary. The doctor went straight to the hospital to get things prepared and at ten o'clock in the evening I followed in a car with Khaled. Gamal came at one in the morning, with members of the Council, to see Khaled after his operation.

I stayed with Khaled in the hospital for eight days. Gamal would come and visit him daily for a few minutes. Mohamed Naguib also came and visited Khaled in the hospital and brought him a box of chocolates, which I threw away and would not let anyone eat. It was Mohamed Naguib who had been behind the attempt on Gamal's life: he was later tried and sentenced to prison. He did not go to prison, but was put under house arrest at the house of Zeinab al-Wakil in al-Marg on the instructions of Gamal. He was released a few years later.

NEWS OF THE PREMIERSHIP
FROM MOHAMED HASSANEIN HEIKAL

I was sound asleep one night when the telephone rang. On answering, I heard the voice of Mohamed Hassanein Heikal on the other

---

8   The assassination attempt at al-Manshiya Square took place on 26 October 1954, ten days after the signing of the treaty of evacuation with the British. The Muslim Brotherhood, which had been dissolved since 14 January 1954 and opposed the regime, planned the assassination attempt in protest against the treaty. Mohamed Naguib, president at the time, was implicated in the plot.

end, saying, "Congratulations. Gamal Abdel Nasser is now prime minister." "Again!" I said. He laughed, saying, "I ring you up to congratulate you on Gamal Abdel Nasser being appointed prime minister and you say, 'Again'?" Gamal had held the post before for a short while and then due to problems had stepped down for Mohamed Naguib.[9] Heikal continued, "I wanted to let you know before he came home. He's on his way."

---

9   Gamal Abdel Nasser was prime minister briefly in early 1954, and again from October 1954 until he assumed the presidency in June 1956.

At Home
after the Revolution

ABDEL HAKIM'S BIRTH

On 8 January 1955, my youngest son, Abdel Hakim, was born. Before going to the hospital to give birth, I called Gamal to let him know. He had a meeting at the house with a Sudanese delegation. He told me that they would leave quickly and he could come with me, but I refused, telling him I could go alone and not to worry. At eleven at night, after I had given birth to my son, the doctor called Gamal to congratulate him and give him the good news. Gamal said, "I will come to the hospital now." The doctor told him that everything was fine and he could wait till morning, but Gamal said, "I always went with her to the hospital and was by her side to congratulate her. I will come now." At midnight, Gamal came to the hospital to see me and his newborn son, who he named Abdel Hakim. He had said before, during the pregnancy, that if it was a boy he would name him Abdel Hakim.

SUMMER 1955

Before the British evacuation from Egypt, we used to get invited to dinner with foreigners.[10] Gamal used to attend and apologize on my

---

10 The British withdrew from Egypt on 18 June 1956, and Nasser raised the
     Egyptian flag at the building of the Suez Canal in Port Said.

behalf, telling me that some of the ladies had asked to meet me and an appointment would be set for another date for us to get acquainted.

I found difficulty in conversing in English, and decided to take steps to learn it properly. I bought books and, with the help of an English teacher, I started using the time that Gamal was out of the house to study English. He would often come home late at night and find me still poring over the books, and we would laugh. As for French, I found that the years I had studied French at school were a great help and I did not have any trouble conversing in that language, and I also used books to help me practice it.

In the summer of 1955, after Gamal's return from the Bandung Conference,[11] an American lady, Mrs. Fleur Cowles, paid him a visit at the house in Manshiyat al-Bakri. She was married to the owner of *Look* magazine. After the meeting, she asked to meet with me and to see the children, and took our photograph with Gamal. This photograph, which I have kept until today, was published in *Time* magazine and some French magazines, and it was the first published photograph of Gamal Abdel Nasser with his family.

That same summer, we went to Alexandria. This time we rented a villa alone, two floors built on high rocks. I used to go to the beach, often to a cabin in Sidi Bishr, where Abdel Hakim played at my side. Gamal came rarely and never spent more than two days. He did not go to the beach at all, but spent the short time with us at the villa.

Summer was over and we returned to Cairo in September. Since the Revolution, I had not been out with Gamal, for there was simply no time. My own outings were rare, and I went to the theater and cinema that I loved, and sometimes to the opera when there was a foreign performer, and to Umm Kulthum's concerts. I would invite as a companion one of my relatives or the wife of one of the officers. Gamal used to tell me, "Go out and have a nice time." He would

---

11 Nasser adopted a policy of non-alignment, between the West and the East. The Bandung Conference was a meeting of non-aligned African and Asian states organized in April 1955.

seem pleased when he knew I had planned an outing, saying, "Keep yourself busy and entertained. It's important that you are happy."

JOVANKA BROZ TITO

In December 1955, President Josip Broz Tito and his wife Jovanka visited Egypt. At the time, women in Egypt did not attend the state banquets and so I invited Jovanka Tito and her accompanying delegation to the house in Manshiyat al-Bakri, along with the wives of the Egyptian ministers.

Jovanka asked to see the children. She was very kind and tender, and loved children. She especially wanted to see Abdel Hakim, who was eleven months old at the time, and she carried him and kissed him. To this day, she remembers Abdel Hakim and first meeting him, and is very fond of him. Whenever she visited us she would always greet him warmly and ask him to sit next to her, and she always invited us to visit them in Yugoslavia.

I also went to visit her at the Qubba Palace alone; she was the first guest I visited there. During this visit, President Tito came into the salon and spent some time talking with us.

The Nationalization of the Suez Canal Company

In the summer of 1956, we rented the same villa in Alexandria that we had the summer before. I returned to Cairo to attend the 23 July celebrations, and on 25 July went back to Alexandria.

On 26 July, the President came to Alexandria to give a speech at al-Manshiya Square. After greeting me, he told me that he was having a cabinet meeting at the house. I left the house before he did, to go and wait for him to give the speech, at a building close to the square. I sat on the balcony, and waited to see him and listen to the speech. Gamal Abdel Nasser came and gave his historic speech.[12]

After I went home, the President arrived with many guests, until the ground floor of the villa was full of people. He did not sleep that night and was on the telephone most of the time. He later told me that the ministers—who had convened at the house for a meeting—had been unaware of the nationalization plans; only two of them knew of his intentions. He told me about the code word "De Lesseps." I told him that I had heard him repeat the word several times and had wondered what it was all about until I heard the

---

12 In his speech at al-Manshiya Square on 26 July 1956, Nasser announced the nationalization of the Suez Canal Company.

big surprise, when his resonant, powerful voice rang out with the decision of the President of the Republic to nationalize the Suez Canal Company.

He spent two work-filled days in Alexandria before going back to Cairo.

CHANGES TO THE HOUSE
AT MANSHIYAT AL-BAKRI

The house at Manshiyat al-Bakri did not undergo any changes until 1956. In August of that year we started to build a second floor, so that the first floor would be an office, two salons, and a dining room, while the second floor would have bedrooms, a study room for the children, a sitting room, and a family dining room.

I stayed with the children in Alexandria while the President was in Cairo, either staying at the Nile Barrages or at the Council headquarters in al-Gezira. I came back at the start of the school year, but the building was not yet finished and so we stayed at the Barrages. At the end of September, we decided to move closer to the children's school and so we stayed at al-Tahra Palace until the renovations on the house were completed.

The President was not happy staying at the palace, saying he was uncomfortable and did not like palaces or life in palaces. He would ask the secretary for daily updates on Manshiyat al-Bakri, pushing for the work to be finished as soon as possible. We stayed at al-Tahra Palace until 27 October, when we returned to our house at Manshiyat al-Bakri.

The President said on our return, "The dining-room furniture has been changed. That table was very dear to me and held many memories. I sat at that table and worked for hours in the period leading up to 23 July." And he wondered, "What have they done with it?"

THE TRIPARTITE AGGRESSION[13]

October 29, 1956 was the birthday of Abdel Hamid. The President was home in his study, and he had asked me to call him when the children arrived for the party; he enjoyed attending his children's birthday parties. He came into the dining room and greeted the children. He stayed a few minutes while we blew out the candles on the cake—Abdel Hamid was five—and then he went back to his study. I was still busy on the first floor with a houseful of children when I met him in the hallway, and he told me he had a meeting and went out.

On 31 October, the British and French attack came, when the President was at home. He asked me to take the children down to the first floor while he went up onto the roof of the house to see the planes, then went into his study and stayed there. I stayed for two days on the first floor, where he had sorted out sleeping arrangements for us, while he slept on the second floor and left the house daily, coming back late each night. A bomb was dropped close to our house, and shrapnel and debris were scattered in the garden. All the residents of the area had left.

Before he left the next morning he told me, "I have the responsibility for the country and its sons and daughters; you have the responsibility for our children. Salah al-Shahed will come and take you to a safe house far from this area, at noon." He did not know at the time where we were going exactly.

We went to a small house in Zamalek, only one floor and a basement, with a small unkempt garden. I had never seen a house in Zamalek like this one; the rooms and the furnishings were old and strange. I asked Salah al-Shahed, "Who did this house belong to?" and he told me, "It belonged to a princess who lives abroad and doesn't use it."

---

13 On 29 October 1956 Israel attacked Egypt in Sinai, then the British and the French issued an ultimatum to Egypt to withdraw west of the Suez Canal. When Nasser refused, the British and the French attacked and invaded Port Said. The United Nations Security Council ended the war on 6 November.

I called the President on the telephone and we spoke for a while, and he asked about the children. I called him the following day as well. On the third day when I called, Zakaria Mohieddin answered and told me that the President was not at the Council and that he would call me when he was back. I became very worried until finally I reached him on the phone and heard his voice. I knew then that he had been on his way to Port Said.

Five days after my arrival at the house in Zamalek, the President called me on the telephone—the hostilities had stopped just hours before—and he told me that I could go back to our house at Manshiyat al-Bakri.

I found the area of Manshiyat al-Bakri deserted, its residents having not yet returned. I called Gamal daily on the telephone while he remained at the Revolutionary Command Council. At the end of each phone call he would say his usual words, "Do you want anything?" and I would thank him and say no. After a week, I asked him when he was coming home and he replied, "When the British leave Egypt." The following day, when he asked me his usual question, "Do you want anything?" I told him, "I want the British to leave Egypt." And we laughed.

Three weeks later, I received a telephone call telling me that the President was on his way home. It was ten in the evening and the children were asleep when he arrived. He had a cold and a fever, and told me that the doctor had insisted that he return home, saying that staying at the Council was not helping his influenza or his fever.

Life at Manshiyat al-Bakri after the Evacuation

The house has two floors. The ground floor has a first entrance into a sitting area, then an entrance to the left to the President's study and an entrance to the right to the President's private salon. The house facing ours had been rented to serve as offices for the guards and secretaries.

The President worked from home more often, using his study and salon for meetings, and the activity in the house increased. I could detect no difference between mornings and nights; even when I had been out and came home late from the theater or opera, I would find the house as it had been before I left, a beehive of activity with all the lights on in the ground floor.

The President took a keen interest in his children's education and, even though he was so busy, he found the time to see their report cards each month and to compare them with the month before. He would call in the children and talk to them about their results.

I never found the opportune moment to give him the report cards, and so I would place them open on a table in the bedroom with a pen so he could sign. The children's results, however, were thankfully always good. Hoda always came first in her class, with a wide gap between her and the second place, while Khaled always came either first or second, having a healthy competition with one of his classmates, which used to amuse Gamal. He would tell me that our greatest legacy to our children was knowledge.

The President had no time to choose his clothes; he would ask the secretary to bring in samples of fabric, and I would try to find time in his busy schedule to show them to him. Once he had made a choice, a tailor would be called in. The tailor always had a problem getting an appointment with the President for a fitting. Once, he went ahead and finished the suit without a fitting; obviously it was useless and was never worn, and so he learned to wait—no matter how long—until the President was free for a fitting.

His pajamas were all similar in color, and I knew he preferred light pastel stripes. Knowing his taste, I managed to choose the fabric for him, but, again, after they were made the size was sometimes not correct and they would have to be taken back for alterations. I met the tailor once in the ground floor sitting room with the children, and he asked me about the latest pajamas and told me that he really needed to take the President's measurements again. The President was getting dressed in the bedroom when I told him about the man's request, and he promised to pass by him in the sitting room on his way out. As for new shoes, I would place them beside the chair he sat on before going out. He would tell me that he did not have the time to choose, and so I would put them back in the boxes. His secretary would keep asking me about the shoes, and I would have to keep repeating the process.

EATING HABITS AT THE HOUSE

We did not have set meal times at all; we could have lunch at two, or three, or even after four. I would wait for the President to come up from the ground floor for us to have lunch together, and he would always ask why I had not gone ahead and had my lunch without him. He always asked for the children to sit at the table with him, whether they had already eaten or not, and the children generally ate when they came back from school.

As for breakfast, he would have it sent up to the bedroom before he went out. Sometimes he would be in too much of a hurry and would only have a glass of milk or juice. He always asked for me to come and sit with him while he had his breakfast, even if I had already eaten.

As for supper, he would generally have it alone, unless the time was not too late and we ate together. He always had a light supper of cheese, yoghurt, and fruit, and he preferred white cheese.

We did not have a wide choice for meals, usually vegetables with rice, and either meat, poultry, or fish.

My daughter Mona did not eat fish and so meat would be prepared for her. Once a week, we had a meal without meat or poultry. The President believed that one day our children would have a life of their own and that they should not feel a difference between the life they led with us and whatever the future held for them, and this would make them happier people. I was totally convinced of his opinions and carried out his instructions to the letter.

THE CHILDREN

He was not unduly strict with the children. He used to tell me that a child who was beaten would protect himself by lying, and as he grew up would make a habit of lying; and so the most important thing was to teach a child never to lie and to guide them. Whenever one of our children did something wrong, he would explain the right conduct. He had the patience to keep guiding them to the right path, no matter how many times the wrong deed was repeated.

Presidential Duties

YUGOSLAVIA, 1958

The union with Syria was in February 1958,[14] and the President was burdened with work. He traveled to Syria for a month and I remained in Cairo.

In the summer of 1958, he was invited to Yugoslavia and President Tito insisted that the children and I accompany him on the visit. I traveled to Alexandria with the children ahead of the President, and we took *al-Hurriya* to Yugoslavia on my first trip abroad. We were accompanied by Dr. Mahmoud Fawzi, the foreign minister, and Mohamed Hassanein Heikal, and their wives.

When we arrived at the port of Dubrovnik, we were received by President Tito and his wife. It was the first time for me to see or be part of an official reception. There was music playing that stopped and started as we made our way along. The President would murmur instructions to me to take steps forward and to stop, as I walked by his side, so that I would not make any mistakes. Under his guidance it all went well and my nervousness vanished.

The two delegations had lunch together, and at night the President and his delegation traveled with President Tito to attend ·a

---

14 On 22 February 1958, Egypt and Syria united to form the United Arab
   Republic. In September 1961, Syria, led by Baathists, withdrew from the union.

celebration of a Yugoslav official holiday, while I remained with Jovanka Tito and the ladies in Dubrovnik for two days.

The two presidents returned and we left Dubrovnik to sail to the island of Veliki Brijun. As we got off the ship, there was another formal reception awaiting us. This time, as I walked beside the President and he turned to murmur instructions, he found me keeping pace on my own. Alone at night he told me, "You have learned." And I replied, "I got to recognize the music!"

We spent two days on the island and then drove by car around the beautiful country of Yugoslavia. I had some nervous moments on the trip. At each constituent republic we visited we were received by the president of the republic, as was their custom. I remember on one occasion, before leaving one morning, the President told me that the president of the republic, who had not been present to welcome us, would be present to see us off, and I needed to shake hands with him. In the foyer of the hotel I saw a man standing who I had not seen before and so I shook hands with him. At that moment, President Tito approached accompanied by another man I had not met before, and Gamal leaned toward me and whispered, "Shake hands with President Tito and the man beside him." At night he laughed and told me, "I asked you to shake hands with the president and I found you shaking hands with the maître d'hôtel first." I told him, "You said to shake hands with the man I had not seen before." We laughed as I promised not to make the same mistake again.

The next day, we moved on to a new place. The two presidents rode together in a car and I rode with the first lady. On arrival, I noticed that three men were waiting for us at the entrance to the hotel. The two presidents alighted before us and I could not see who they shook hands with first. When the time came for me, I made my choice only to be told by Gamal at night that I had chosen the secretary to shake hands with, and again we laughed.

The day after, the President did not give me any comments and so I told him, "You see, I made no mistakes today and so we have nothing to laugh about."

One week into our trip to Yugoslavia, the revolution in Iraq broke out. We set sail for Alexandria from Brijun, even though it was dangerous due to the American fleet's presence in the Mediterranean. We had not yet left the Adriatic when a telegram arrived from President Tito warning us that the situation was too dangerous for us to continue.

At night, I was with the children and the wife of Dr. Mahmoud Fawzi watching a film in the onboard cinema when the ship stopped. When the film ended I got up to go to my room and met Heikal on the deck of the ship. He said, "I want to ask you one question. The situation is very critical; President Tito is warning of the danger of continuing the trip and the ship has stopped moving. The President is in the command post receiving news and telegrams, and you are watching a film. It is one of two things: either I am a coward or you are extremely brave." I replied, "Neither. I have just gotten used to critical situations." He said, "I am not worried about myself: I am worried about President Gamal Abdel Nasser. It is him the Americans want." I said, "God willing, he will come to no harm."

The ship remained still until morning, and the President had worked through the night. In the morning, he left the ship to board one of the two destroyers that accompanied us together with Dr. Fawzi and Heikal. The women, children, and remaining delegation sailed back to Brijun.

We arrived the next day and were taken to the hospitality villa. President Tito asked to see me the next day in his villa close by. He told me, "President Gamal Abdel Nasser is now in the Soviet Union, outside Moscow. The visit and its location are top secret. Your presence in Brijun will also be kept secret and you will remain in the villa and not go out so that nobody knows your whereabouts. I will give you news when I receive it."

For two days we stayed in the villa without going out. The delegation included security as well as the doctor. They resided in the basement, a few steps down from the first floor. When any of them tried to go out they were prevented by the guards at the doors. The head of security asked to meet with me. "We are like prisoners here," he said. "Do you know where the President is? We are worried about him." I tried to put the man's mind at ease, telling him the President was safe and that President Tito would pass on the news as it came to him.

Jovanka Tito used to visit us each day and stay until the evening. The ladies were all very worried, especially the wife of Mohamed Hassanein Heikal, who was in tears. We listened to the radio and finally heard news that President Gamal Abdel Nasser and his accompanying delegation had reached Syria.

At last we were allowed out and President Tito took us on a voyage on a yacht. We learned that President Gamal Abdel Nasser had arrived in Cairo on a Soviet plane. The same plane landed in Brijun to take us back to Egypt. It was the first time I had flown in an airplane.

We were scheduled to arrive on 22 July, and the President was giving a speech that night. He was working in his study, asking for information from the secretary about when the plane had left and when it was expected to arrive. He told the secretary to let him know as soon as our plane had landed. The expected time came and went, and two hours passed. Later, the president told me that he had put down his pen and had been overcome by worry, calculating how long the trip should take and how much fuel we had. When the time came for him to leave the house and to give his speech, as he approached the waiting vehicle he saw the officer running toward him with news that we had landed at Inshas Airport. Cairo Airport was not equipped at the time to land the fighter jet plane.

Gamal told me, "Waiting for you was one of the hardest times of my life and the most worrying." We later learned that he had been told that we were on the plane two hours before we had actually boarded.

TOGETHER IN A CAR

We were at the rest house at the Barrages and planned on driving back home in the evening. I used to ride in the same car as the children and the President used to go alone in his car, preferring us to move before him. While we were sitting together in the garden, I told him, "It's been years since I've been with you in a car." He said, "Ride back with me today." When we were ready to leave, I walked with him toward the waiting car. The officer standing next to the car acknowledged me and then headed toward my car to open the door for me. A look of confusion came over his face when he realized that I had not followed him and had gotten into the President's car. I told the President, "You see how shocked they are? Six years and they've never seen us together in a car!"

There was no time for him to actually spend with me, but he liked me by his side while he was at home or in his room. If he came into the house or up from his study and did not find me waiting for him, he would say, "I looked everywhere for you." He would sometimes go into the children's rooms and play with them for a few minutes. I never saw him rest; his time was taken up with reading, or writing, or on the telephone. The only time he was not working was while he was sleeping.

I would listen to him talking on the telephone and not utter a word or comment, no matter how critical or important the conversation seemed to be. The dossiers that were delivered to him I would put on the table in his room ready for him. While in his room, he would receive messages and memos, and he would give instructions over the phone or in writing to his secretary. The international newspapers would be brought to him daily and he would read them all. For days I might not find the time to talk with him, but he would always greet me and acknowledge me whenever he saw me.

hia hosts a reception for the wives of heads of state of Asian nations, 10 January 1958

With President Tito of Yugoslavia and his wife Jovanka on Veliki Brijun, 8 July 1958

With the president of Mexico, Adolfo Ruiz Cortines, November 1958

...hia with the family of Emperor Haile Selassie of Ethiopia, Manshiyat al-Bakri, 27 June 1959

Welcoming Norodom Sihanouk, prime minister of Cambodia, 20 November 1959

the state visit to Greece, with King Paul and Queen Frederika, 6 June 1960

The official visit of Crown Prince Constantine of Greece, Manshiyat al-Bakri, 14 April 196

On a boat on the Nile with the Titos, January 1961

Welcoming the prime minister of Burma, U Nu, at Cairo Airport, 24 December 1961

ahia with U Nu's wife Mya Yi

The official visit of Princess Margarethe of Denmark, 15 November 1962

...hia hosts a dinner reception for the wives of heads of state attending the Africa ...mmit Meeting in Cairo, 16 June 1962

dinner reception for Hamani Diori, president of the Republic of Niger, 7 May 1963

Tahia escorts Marie-Thérèse Houphouët-Boigny, wife of the president of Côte d'Ivoire, at a reception in the Qubba Palace, 14 July 1963

eceiving the premier of the Republic of China, Zhou Enlai, 14 December 1963

Tahia and Mona Abdel Nasser with Nina Khrushcheva, wife of the Russian premier, Alexandria, 9 May 1964

The President and his wife wait to welcome President Tito of Yugoslavia to the Non-Aligned Movement Summit Cairo, October 1964

With Jawaharlal Nehru, prime minister of India, and Josip Broz Tito, president of Yugoslavia

Welcoming Queen Ratna of Nepal at Cairo Airport, 4 October 1964

President Nasser hands out land deeds to farmers

he President speaks at a Revolutionary rally, accompanied by Abdel Hakim Amer and alah Salem

efore the rift:
Iasser with General
Iohamed Naguib,
gypt's first president

vacuation talks with the British, 1954

On the train en route to Alexandria

resident Nasser in Damascus, celebrating the second anniversary of the union with
yria, February 1960

Greeting soldiers returning from Yemen, 1963

In Tsqaltubo, 1968

t the front during the War of Attrition with minister of defense, Mohamed Fawzi, 1968

President Nasser is sworn into office for a new term by Anwar al-Sadat, speaker of the National Assembly, March 1965

With the future president of Cyprus, Archbishop Makarios III, 1958

'ith Fidel Castro, prime minister of Cuba, June 1959

With US president Dwight D. Eisenhower, 1960

With Ahmed Ben Bella, first president of Algeria, May 1963

With future US president Richard Nixon and his wife Pat, 23 June 1963

With Che Guevara, 1965

With boxing brothers Muhammad Ali and Rahman Ali, May 1966

With future president Anwar al-Sadat and 'Star of the East' Umm Kulthum, Day of Knowledge, 1966

With King Faisal of Saudi Arabia and PLO chairman Yasser Arafat, the Arab League Summit, 1970

بسم الله الرحمن الرحيم

اليوم ٢٤ سبتمبر ١٩٧٤ ، أى بعد أربعة أيام
يكون الذكرى الثالث لرحيل القائد الخالد جمال عبدالناصر
زوجى الحبيب ، لم تمر على دقائقه إلا وأنا حزينة وهو
أمام عينای فی کل لحظه عشتها معه ، صوته ، صورته
المشرقة ، إنسانيته ، كفاحه ، جهاده ، كلامه ، أقواله ،
خطبه ، أى من الذكريات أبكى بالدموع أو أحبسه بالبكاء
وهى إذا ضغطت شعورى أى خنقة بالبكاء مستمر.
لقد عشت مع جمال عبدالناصر ثمانى سنوات قبل
قيامه بالثورة وثمانى عشر عاما بعد نجاحه للثورة
فى ٢٣ يوليو ١٩٥٢ ، فقد تزوجنا فى ٢٩ يونيو ١٩٤٤
أى عشت معه ستة وعشرون عاما وثلاثة أشهر

When we returned from Alexandria in the fall of 1958, the President found out that he had diabetes. This news saddened me greatly, and I would go down and sit alone in the garden and weep. I stopped eating sweets myself for a long time, and would never serve anything at home that was forbidden in his diet. He used to say, "Thank God, diabetes is much milder than other illnesses." Out of extreme caution and worry over his health, I took to cooking all his meals myself.

DINING WITH AN EMPEROR

In February 1959, the President traveled to Syria during the union celebrations and stayed for a month while I remained in Cairo.

In June 1959, I attended my first state dinner with the President, held for Emperor Haile Selassie of Ethiopia and attended by all the ministers and their wives, and the diplomatic corps.

I stood next to the President and the emperor, and received the guests. While sitting down for dinner, I felt a quickening of my heartbeat and felt I was about to faint. I whispered my predicament to the President, who told me to go into the study and rest. We were at the Qubba Palace and a doctor was sent for. The President remained with his guests until the event was over and we went home. The next day, he ordered a medical check-up. I was pronounced in good health and the diagnosis was a case of nerves about my first official dinner with an emperor.

At another dinner, this time with Prime Minister Nehru of India, I was seated between the President and our guest. Prime Minister Nehru kept up a lively conversation with me. During dinner, I started feeling the same: my heart beat faster and I felt dizzy, and I remembered the dinner with Haile Selassie. I decided to stay in my place and not mention anything to the President, even if my heart stopped. Toward the end of the dinner, while dessert was being served, I started to feel well again. When we finished, I was able to get up and walk side-by-side with the President and Prime Minister Nehru.

On our way home, Gamal told me, "I noticed that you weren't yourself during dinner, and I decided not to mention anything so you wouldn't panic because I had noticed, and so I talked to the lady sitting next to me." I told him what had happened to me and how I had decided to handle it. The next day, he ordered another medical check-up, and the doctor told me, "You have managed to cure yourself. It probably won't happen to you again." He gave me some pills to take to calm my nerves before official events, and I took them for a time. But there were so many official events that I soon got used to them and did not need any medicine. At some events, I was even required to give out medals, which doubled the official duties for me.

A STATE VISIT TO GREECE

In the summer of 1960, the President received an invitation from President Tito for us all to spend the summer in Yugoslavia on the island of Veliki Brijun. At the same time he had received an official invitation to visit Greece and I was invited with him. And so the decision was made for us to go to Greece on our way to Yugoslavia. The head of security traveled ahead of us to Greece and met with the Greek head of protocol, who told him that in Greece it was the custom for both men and women to wear evening dress for state dinners. The man came back to Egypt and told the President, who replied that he was not going to wear evening dress and that he would cancel the visit to Greece. When this reply was passed on to the head of Greek protocol, the response came back that the king of Greece welcomed Gamal Abdel Nasser dressed however he chose to be, as long as he came to Greece.

We boarded *al-Hurriya* with the children and the foreign minister, Dr. Mahmoud Fawzi, and Mohamed Hassanein Heikal, and their wives. When we docked, the king and queen and their children, the crown prince and his two sisters, were there to receive us in a boat that took us to land, where there was a formal reception. Cars took us to the palace where we would reside; the President rode with the king and I rode with the queen.

That night, the king held a formal banquet and invited members of the royal family, the prime minister, and the cabinet. The guests stood on the two sides of the banqueting hall to greet us as we passed down the middle, as was the royal custom. The queen walked beside the President and tried to take his arm. He told her, "I will walk beside the king and you can walk beside my wife." The queen said, "But what if I were to take your arm?" And he told her, "I would be very embarrassed." The queen stepped back and stood at my side, and told me in English, "I will take your arm instead of your husband's." And we walked down the hall, greeted on both sides by the guests.

End of the Union

The President used to travel to Syria for the union celebrations each year and stay for more than a month. I never went with him, since he preferred that I remain with the children.

On the morning of 28 September 1961, the President received an urgent phone call. I was standing by his side at the time. He was informed of a military coup in Syria, and told that Abdel Hakim Amer was there. He quickly rose and got dressed, and went out, extreme agitation showing on his face. I remained quiet and did not comment on the news. I heard his speech on the radio and sensed how distressed he was, and I felt for his sadness. But the truth was, I was not upset by the separation from Syria. After giving the speech he came back home, still very distressed, and then he went out again and I followed the news on the radio.

I had mixed emotions: should I be upset or not? The union had not been a source of comfort to me. It increased the President's burdens and in the last few years—since 1958 to be exact—he had become diabetic, and I was convinced it was due to the pressure and excessive work as well as his annual long trip to Syria, during which we were parted.

The President came home that night and I was with him in the room; neither of us spoke a word, and I still had not decided if I was upset or not.

That summer in Alexandria, we were at Maamoura, where two identical houses had been built in 1959 for the President and Abdel Hakim Amer. Amer's house later became the resort used by President Anwar al-Sadat when he was in Maamoura. The Field Marshal sat with the President on the beach, and I sat beside them as they talked about Syria and the separation. The President nodded toward me, saying, "She is a separatist and did not approve of the union," and they both laughed. Since he had hit on the truth, I laughingly conceded his point, saying, "It was a heavy burden; better that it ended."

As I have said, while the President was at home on the second floor, I was always at his side morning or night. He worked continuously, in the bedroom, in the study, lying down on the bed. I would listen to his telephone calls; sometimes the caller was Mohamed Hassanein Heikal. I noticed that parts of the President's conversations with him were included in Heikal's weekly Friday column in *al-Ahram* newspaper.

The Family Man

President Gamal Abdel Nasser enjoyed watching films and considered this to be his time of rest and relaxation. During a movie, he would still receive memos, and he would read them using a lighter and write his replies in minutes, and then go back to his film. Sometimes, after reading a memo, he would get up and go to his study. Before leaving the room, he would tell me to go on watching, but I always asked for the film to be stopped till he returned. At other times, if he was going to be detained, he would let me know. I could finish the movie if I liked or go back up to the second floor if I was not interested. In the last couple of years, when he had stopped smoking, he used to bring a small flashlight with him to read the memos.

The President enjoyed both taking still photographs and making movies. The rare times he was free, he would go into the garden and ask the children to join him, and take their photographs or film them. I would tell him that he was not in the photographs with us, and so he would ask me to take a photograph of him with the children, and then ask one of the children to take a photograph of us together. He gave each of his children both a regular and a movie camera; he never forgot their birthdays and was always keen on their gifts. He liked music and enjoyed listening to Umm Kulthum; he acquired her recordings, and sometimes made a recording himself, and would listen to the music turned down while he worked.

Although he worked constantly, and in reality did not have time for his family—the children and myself—he still managed to make us feel he was with us at all times and that we were the most important thing in his life.

He was given a very beautiful desk set that included a picture frame. He asked me to arrange the set on top of his desk in his study. Later, I found that he had taken a photograph of me that had been on a table in the study and put it in the frame on the desk, facing him at all times. I thanked him, and I was so happy. The frame still stands in the same place today.

He traveled often; most of his trips were to conferences and I never accompanied him. He would say that he did not want us both on the same plane with the children left behind. Later, I also comprehended that he considered it to be a form of luxury that he was against, being a firm believer in self-sacrifice, and, having understood this, I never asked to accompany him. He would bid me a fond farewell and I would follow the news until the day he returned, which was always a happy day.

The President only accepted gifts from leaders or kings, and he preferred them to be symbolic gifts rather than gifts of value. He was given cars—especially from the Arab kings and princes—a plane, horses, and a boat, all of which he handed over to the state. After his death, he only had in his name our black Austin car, which I was told they wanted to put in a military museum. He was also given many watches by Arab kings, which he always gifted to officers, telling me, "These men were by my side on 23 July."

A rich Arab businessman gave a valuable gift of jewelry to Salah al-Shahed, the chief of security, to give to the President. When presented with the gift, the President refused it and told Salah to take it back. The businessman entreated Salah to try again with the President. Salah came back to the President, telling him, "The gift is worth more than 100,000 Egyptian pounds." This time the President insisted even more strongly that he would not accept the gift, saying, "I did not lead the Revolution for money or jewels. I could issue a decree to increase my salary tenfold if I wanted to, but that is not what I undertook a revolution for. Take it back. I do not want to see it." Salah went back to the businessman, who finally sent a Parker pen, hoping that the President would accept it, which he did. When the President told me the story, he said, "Salah annoyed me."

When our daughter Hoda came to be married, a cabinet member sent a gift of jewelry that Gamal refused and returned. A friend of Hoda's was the daughter of an ambassador, and she gave her a diamond-encrusted watch, which her father told her to return with a thank-you letter.

SONS, DAUGHTERS, AND GRANDCHILDREN

Hoda passed her final year at school with distinction and was accepted at the Faculty of Economics and Political Science at Cairo University. She was one of the students with whom the President shook hands on Knowledge Day, 1963, and was presented with a prize and a certificate of merit.

Hoda met Hatem Sadek, a fellow student, in the third year at university. She told me about him, and said that they used to meet during sports practice—Hoda played basketball—and that he had spoken to her of his wish to formally propose after his graduation. I instructed her never to meet him outside of university and did not mention the issue to the President.

The following year, when Hoda was in her second year and Hatem in his fourth year, she asked me to tell her father. I told her that I would, but found that she had already spoken to him before I did. Her father wished her well and told me, "She says that his father is retired from the Ministry of Agriculture and that they live on al-Haram Street." This was the same information that I had also received from Hoda.

The President went on to say, "When the time is closer to the engagement, I will ask about the family." He went on, "This is what I want for my daughters, to choose the men they wish to marry." He added, "I have received many requests for their hands in marriage from sons of wealthy businessmen and former pashas, but I have always refused." He used to send his thanks with his personal secretary.

Before the end of the academic year in 1964, Hoda told me that Hatem Sadek wished to come and formally propose. It was a few days before exams, but he wanted to come because he was about to graduate and they would not be seeing each other at university any more. I informed the President, who told me to set up an appointment to receive him and his mother—he added that he would not ask about the family since they were already in agreement. What purpose would it serve?

Hatem and his mother came and met me and Hoda. After the visit, I asked the President to set a time to meet the father, and he did. After the two fathers met, the President came upstairs to the second floor and told me, "Congratulations. The marriage ceremony will be in two weeks." "Why so soon?" I asked. He said, "I told him we were from Upper Egypt and did not believe in an engagement period. It will be a marriage ceremony."

Hoda finished her third year at university and in the summer of 1965, on 5 August, after her exams, we had the wedding. She still had one more year to go at university. After the wedding and after the guests had left, and we had bid Hoda farewell—her father kissing her and crying—we went upstairs to the second floor. He was very emotional and said, "Hoda has left us." The next evening, he still seemed overwhelmed with Hoda leaving the house and I told him, "She chose Hatem and she loves him. She is happy." He said, "I wish her happiness. She is now living her own life."

In 1966, Hoda graduated with merit and distinction, and was hired as a member of the presidential staff alongside her husband, Hatem Sadek.

The year after Hoda had gone to university, Mona had passed her last year at school. Although she wished to join her sister at the Faculty of Economics and Political Science at Cairo University, she did not have the required grades. The minister of higher education and the university expressed their readiness to accept Mona, but her father would not accept any favors for his daughter. Consequently, she joined the Faculty of Economics and Political Science at the American University in Cairo.

Ashraf Marawan, a young officer in the army, in the chemicals division, proposed to Mona. His father was also a military man. Mona had met him with his sister, who was an acquaintance of hers at the club. The marriage process followed the same path as her sister's, and the wedding took place after her second-year exams, on 7 July 1966.

Hoda gave birth to Hala, the President's first grandchild. When her husband called me to tell me the news of the birth—it was at night—I rushed over to the hospital with her brothers. When I returned home, I found the President in the bedroom. As soon as I walked in, he said, "Greetings to the grandmother." How wonderful to be called grandmother for the first time! The following morning, he went and visited Hoda in the hospital, and carried his granddaughter in his arms. He was photographed and the picture was published in the newspapers, and I have kept it.

Three months later, Mona gave birth to a son. Again, the President visited her in the hospital and carried his grandson, and was photographed. The picture of the President carrying Gamal was also published in the newspapers.

Mona finished university and I attended her graduation. I was impressed with the university and enjoyed seeing Mona walk in the procession in her cap and gown. She then worked at Dar al-Maaref publishing house.

Khaled joined the Faculty of Engineering at Cairo University, with a high-school score of 81%. Once busy with his university lectures and studies, he was no longer able to make it to lunch with the family, and his father would ask about him, since they had conflicting schedules, "Where is Khaled? I haven't seen him for days."

1967

THE JUNE WAR

The Israelis had attacked Syria and the President was with us that morning. He said, "The Israelis will attack Egypt." And he indicated the exact day—the following Monday. His prediction came true: Israel attacked on 5 June 1967, in the morning.

On 9 June, the President gave a speech. I was in the sitting room with Abdel Hamid and Abdel Hakim, then twelve years old, watching the speech on television. The President announced that he was stepping down. I had no idea that he intended this, and I could see the sadness on his face. I looked at my sons and saw the same sadness mirrored in theirs. Khaled, my eldest son, entered the room and I told them, "Your father is a great man and he is now greater, so don't be upset." Abdel Hamid said, "It is better for him to rest." And they got up and left the room.

A few minutes later, I could hear the crowds outside the house. The President returned home, went up to the bedroom, took off his suit and put on his pajamas, and lay down on the bed.

The road was blocked with people and many could not reach the house. The first floor was filled with his deputies and ministers, and officers. Many of them were crying openly, some sitting on the stairs weeping and asking to be allowed into his room. I would go in and inform him of those who wanted to meet him. He allowed in very few—maybe three or four—and I saw them come out weeping. He then got dressed in his suit and went down to the first floor to meet with them all for a short time. When he came up to the bedroom again, he got into bed, took a sedative, and told me that he would sleep. Mohamed Allouba, his personal attendant, knocked on the door, carrying some memos and dossiers, and the President told me to tell him to take them and go away. I remained at his side, hearing the crowds growing louder outside the house.

When I woke in the morning, the sound of the crowds was beyond imagination. I usually left the room each morning and would go back when I heard him ring the bell for his attendant. We would wish each other a good morning, and he would start his reading and phone calls. I would then go back again when he asked for his breakfast and spend some time with him. But on that day, I did not go back to the room. He received individual guests all day and remained in the bedroom.

In the afternoon, I saw chairs being formally and precisely lined up in rows in the garden, with a table facing them. I also saw members of the media with their crews, and I asked, "What is this for?" I was told that the National Assembly was going to hold a session. I was beyond surprise for I had seen many strange things in my life and here they were conducting an open-air session of the National Assembly at my home.

I left the verandah where I had been standing watching and went into the house to finish cooking a meal for the President. Mona came in and said to me, "Anwar al-Sadat is announcing on television that father has agreed to remain as President, and you're standing here?" I went into the living room and watched Anwar al-Sadat, who was heading the National Assembly at the time, approaching the end of his speech. "What is the setup in the garden then, and what about the media crews outside?" I asked. I was told that the members of the Assembly were unable to make it to the house due to the crowds filling the streets and that they had therefore convened at the headquarters; all of this while the President remained in his room. I went upstairs and found him lying down, and said nothing.

We remained in Cairo until August, when the President told me to go to Alexandria with the children. He joined us in September, after having exposed a conspiracy by Field Marshal Abdel Hakim Amer, who wanted to return to power by force after recent changes in the military command. [15] A few days later, the President received news that Amer had committed suicide. The news both shocked and saddened him. He returned to Cairo immediately and I followed with the children the following day. I found the President in a state of deep sorrow, mourning his friend Abdel Hakim Amer, and he remained that way for a long time.

The President worked constantly, day and night. At night I would hear the telephone ring, and he would give instructions, then receive feedback. Most of the calls were regarding military maneuvers, and he would wait to hear results. When his instructions were not followed and mistakes happened, he would get extremely agitated and I could see the annoyance on his face.

Memos were also sent to him at any hour of the day or night. At lunch—which, as mentioned before, did not have a specific time—we would wait for him at the table on the second floor, myself and whichever of the children were at home, while he finished off his work in the study. He would come for a few stolen moments to eat his meal before returning to work. If he came to the table very late, he would say, "I'm late. Why did you wait for me?"

SPA TREATMENT

The President felt a pain in his leg that lasted for months, and I did not see him rest or reduce his workload in any way. He met

---

15 Abdel Hakim Amer's resignation had taken place along with Nasser's resignation, but when the people went out in demonstrations for Nasser to remain in office, he had refused the return of Amer, because he sought to introduce major reforms in the Egyptian army.

Mohamed Awad al-Koni (the ambassador to the UN), who told him that he had suffered similar symptoms and had gone to a spa in the Soviet Union to receive treatment in mineral-water baths. The symptoms had receded and, after going again the following year, they had totally disappeared. The President made a visit to the Soviet Union in the summer of 1968, and, before returning to Cairo, he had a medical check-up. They advised him to stop smoking, which he did—his last cigarette was extinguished in the Soviet Union—and told him that a visit to the spa was in order. The President agreed and came back to Cairo.

He told me about it a couple of days after his return and said that he wished me to accompany him on the trip, along with Khaled, Abdel Hamid, and Abdel Hakim.

At the end of July, we boarded the Soviet presidential plane that had been sent to transport us to Georgia. When we landed, the president and his wife were waiting for us and we were taken by car for a half-hour drive to the town of Tsqaltubo. It had three spas for healing with mineral-water baths, a long main road lined with trees and benches, and shops selling refreshments at the end of the road. The whole town catered for patients and their companions, with no residential buildings at all, and it was mostly used by Russians.

A spa was prepared to accommodate the President, who was visited by all the prominent doctors, as well as having a resident doctor to oversee his treatment. The President had expressed his wish for the visit to be for treatment only and that he did not want to meet official visitors.

He organized a trip for our sons to the beaches of the Black Sea and a visit to Moscow. The President would go to the baths each morning, then come back, and we would have breakfast together. In the evenings, the doctors had prescribed a long walk, which he would take with the Egyptian doctor, al-Sawy Habib, the Russian doctor, the Egyptian ambassador, who was staying with us, his personal secretary, and accompanying officers. I would go out for a walk as well, usually with the ambassador's wife, and we would sometimes meet the President and his entourage on our way. I have a picture of me on my walk, meeting the President sitting on one of the benches.

The President received a warm welcome in Tsqaltubo; people would wait to greet him as he went to the baths in the morning or on his evening walk.

At night, after nine o'clock, he would make his calls to Cairo, receiving news and giving instructions, and he would also read all the Arabic newspapers and listen to the radio.

Twenty-three days later, our trip came to an end. The doctors said that the treatment was successful and they expected the pain to remain in the leg for maybe a month more, but then it would gradually decrease until it went away completely. Thank God, this happened, and the President was cured of his ailment.

While bidding me farewell, the Russians told me that although I had visited the Soviet Union, I had seen nothing at all of their country, and they insisted that I repeat the visit. The President promised that I would join him on his next trip.

ABDEL HAMID AT THE NAVAL ACADEMY

In September 1968, Abdel Hamid joined the Naval Academy. It had always been his wish to pursue military studies, and the Naval Academy was his choice.

After the first week of Abdel Hamid's absence, the President told me, "I miss Mido." "Parents visit their children weekly at the Academy," I said. "You can go and visit him if you wish," he replied. The following week I traveled to Alexandria with his brothers. The President had arranged for Abdel Hamid to come out of the academy and meet us at the designated time for visits. We arrived at the academy and I saw an officer waiting by the gates, and we drove on to the end of the academy wall and parked the car. Abdel Hamid came out and met us. His brothers cheered when they saw him in uniform, with a crew cut, and he spent ten happy minutes with us.

At the Nile Barrages on Nasser's last birthday, 15 January 1970

Tahia with Abdel Hamid and Abdel Hakim at Manshiyat al-Bakri

With Mona, Khaled, and Abdel Hamid, 20 May 1956

The house at Manshiyat al-Bakri

the garden of Manshiyat al-Bakri, 1968

he President plays tennis

In the garden of Manshiyat al-Bakri

oda's wedding, 5 August 1965

One week after the birth of the first granddaughter, Hala

With Hala at Manshiyat al-Bakri

With Hoda and Hala in the garden of Manshiyat al-Bakri

With Hala at Manshiyat al-Bakri

the garden of Manshiyat al-Bakri

aying chess with Khaled in the garden of Manshiyat al-Bakri

the garden of Manshiyat al-Bakri with Abdel Hakim and grandson Gamal

Nasser's funeral, 1 October 1970

The Gamal Abdel Nasser Mosque in Manshiyat al-Bakri on the day of Nasser's funeral, 1 October 1970

The tomb inside the Gamal Abdel Nasser Mosque

He was then escorted back into the Academy by the officer. There was a small building by the gate where students at the Academy met their parents.

The President told me, "God willing, we will attend Abdel Hamid's graduation together and see our son a naval officer." I used to visit Abdel Hamid every week for the full period of his initiation as a new recruit, before they are allowed out of the academy. I remember the heavy rain on my very last visit.

Before Abdel Hamid was due for his first visit home, the President told me to arrange for the photographer to come and take our picture welcoming Abdel Hamid home in uniform. Unfortunately, when I informed the President of the time, he was not available and so the picture was taken of me and Abdel Hamid alone in the garden, as he came into the house.

Abdel Hamid graduated on 29 June 1972. I received a visit from the head of the academy to invite me to the graduation and I cried as I accepted the invitation, wishing that the President could be with me as he had promised. I attended the graduation amid a warm welcome from the naval commander at the academy, the minister of defense, and the professors. I was given a silver tray with the shield of the academy and my name engraved on it. I was then invited to tea with the commander and minister, and Officer Abdel Hamid Gamal Abdel Nasser was called into the room to shake my hand. I congratulated him, and they bid me a warm farewell as if I was accompanied by the President himself.

PREOCCUPIED WITH THE ARMED FORCES

The President was extremely busy, his main focus being the armed forces: building a strong army and forcing the Israelis out of Sinai. He would call the commander-in-chief at any time while the armed forces were involved in operations in Sinai, and would not sleep until he had heard the results. I could see the sorrow on his face when there were losses and the peace when they were successful. One afternoon, he learned of the loss of a plane during an air raid and I heard him express his distress at the loss of the pilot.

That night, while I was walking in the garden, he came down to walk with me as he sometimes did before receiving a visitor, and told me, "The pilot was able to parachute himself to safety. I thought I should tell you because I know how upset you were about him." He was right; I did get very upset when I learned of any losses of human life, just as I was pleased at any success in the operations. As usual, I gave no comment.

The President would often ask me to pray for victory in my daily prayers and would tell me to "curse the Israelis."

I would never broach a political subject with him unless he initiated the conversation, which he rarely did. Once I told him, "I only talk about mundane everyday topics, which might annoy you." He replied, "On the contrary. Stay as you are; it entertains and relaxes me to listen to things that do not involve work or politics."

The President remained preoccupied with building the army, obtaining weapons, and training the troops. All conversations I heard were about war and weapons. The guests at the time included heads of friendly nations, and dinner would be held at the house in the large dining room, which we had sometimes used as our cinema at home. The banquet would include the guest and his accompanying delegation, as well as deputies to the President and ministers. I would attend the dinner as well as accompanying the President to receive the guests at the airport, since most of them came with their wives.

The First Heart Attack

When Khaled and Abdel Hakim finished their exams in the summer of 1969, I went with them to Alexandria. It was the President's preference that I accompany them there. He was still worried about them swimming far out to sea. The President remained in Cairo at Manshiyat al-Bakri until August, when he came to Alexandria for a few days. He spent all his time working, in meetings in the salon overlooking the sea or in his study with his dossiers.

He told me that I would be accompanying him on a trip in the first week of September to the Soviet Union. He would go to Moscow first for meetings and then to Tsqaltubo for treatment. The doctors had advised him to return in a year and a house had been built to accommodate him during his stay. The President went back to Cairo and I returned there at the end of August.

At the beginning of September, there was a revolution in Libya, and, as the President was preoccupied with the events, consequently our trip to the Soviet Union was postponed. The leaders of the Libyan Revolution came to Cairo to visit the President and he told me that we would travel by mid-September.

A few days later, the President had a fever and was instructed by his doctors to remain in bed. It was the first heart attack. He did not tell me and gave orders to the doctors to keep the news from me. He told me that he had a bout of influenza. Some days later, I was meeting guests on the ground floor and, when the visit ended, I found some equipment placed by the stairs. When I asked what it was, I was told that they were installing an elevator. It was then that I understood and went upstairs weeping, only to be met by the doctor coming out of the President's room. When I confronted him, he denied the President's heart condition, telling me that it was one of the doctors who suffered from a heart problem, and the elevator was being installed for him. The man was obviously taken by surprise and could think of nothing else to tell me. I went to my room, not wanting the President to notice my tears, and then I went and stayed by his side.

RECOVERY

He spent the day giving his instructions to the armed forces and ministers by telephone. His personal attending doctor, al-Sawy Habib, who resided at the house and gave him his medications, had to wait for the phone calls to finish. Both of us noticed the excessive effort made by the President, even though I did not know the truth in the first days. He used to ask for his meals to be prepared and placed on a small table in his room, and I would sit with him and share the meal. He did not actually lie in bed like other heart patients. He showered and shaved as usual; the only thing he did not do was go into the living room or dining room. He sometimes sat in an armchair placed in his room, but he was not generally in bed.

The attending doctor told the team of specialists treating the President and they advised complete rest, but he carried on as before. Within two weeks, he was calling for meetings in the study adjoining his room and he would work with the visitor in there. After a month, he asked me if the elevator had been installed. I could not hide my anxiety, and he told me, "I know about the elevator. The doctor told me and I gave my permission." In the following month, he started going downstairs for meetings in his study.

After two months, the President finally spoke to me of his illness, saying, "It was a heart attack, but thank God nothing overly serious." I told him that I had known; then I left the room to hide my tears.

Soon after his recovery, the month of Ramadan started. It was the first time for the President not to fast. He would have a light snack in the afternoon and then have his main meal with us at sunset.

BACK TO HEAVY WORK

In January 1970, the President traveled with his doctor and a specialist to Moscow for a short four-day trip.

The President continued working at full speed, going out at nights, meeting with officers at the central command, and staying up late at night just as he had before his illness.

After finishing his meetings on the ground floor, he would ask for his coat and go out. The doctors tried to convince him to slow down, but he would tell them, "I have followed your instructions on treatment and done all you advised, but when it comes to work I cannot do as you say." He went to the front many times and visited the officers and soldiers, remaining there for a couple of days each visit.

Returning from one of his visits, he told me, "I wish I could have stayed, even died there." He had been among the soldiers, many of them volunteering university graduates, fighting in the resistance and playing a vital part in the heroic operations in Sinai.

When the President heard of losses of human lives, he would be greatly distressed. He told me once, "When I see Khaled I can hardly look at him, I feel so sad. He reminds me so much of them. They are so alike." Khaled at the time was a student in the Faculty of Engineering.

The President went to the resort at the Nile Barrages, and on 15 January I took the children and we went to visit him, each bearing a small gift to celebrate his birthday.

He never joined in the celebrations. We would have cakes and candles put on the dining-room table, and he would come downstairs and look at the preparations, smile, and wave at us, then go into his study to work or go out for a meeting. The house would be full of flowers in celebration of his birthday. In the afternoon, we went back to Manshiyat al-Bakri, celebrated his birthday, and put out the candles while he remained at the Barrages for two more days.

In February 1970, we went by train to Aswan. President Tito of Yugoslavia and his wife were paying a visit to Egypt, and had chosen to spend the time in Aswan. We were accompanied by Anwar al-Sadat—who had recently been appointed Vice President—Hussein al-Shafei, Ali Sabri, and their wives. President Tito and his wife stayed for four days and we spent a week before returning to Cairo. The President did not use a plane for traveling in Egypt, preferring to use the train, or a car to Alexandria.

Summer 1970

Abdel Hakim was to take his exams for the second secondary year. The President told him before his exams that if he scored 80% he could ask for any gift, and the secretary, Mohamed Ahmed, would get it for him. Hakim used to wait for any opportunity to enter his father's study, where he would embrace him, and if the President had a camera, radio, or small recorder he would ask Hakim, "What do you think?" And as Hakim left the room he would tell him, "Take it with you."

Hakim passed, and scored 84%, and went into his father's office to tell him the good news. The President congratulated him and said, "Well, what do you want?" Hakim replied, "I don't want anything this year. I want to go to London with Saad al-Serafi." Saad al-Serafi was a pilot and engineer who used to accompany the President on his trips, and Hakim had met him often in the President's office. I was in the room with them at the time and heard the President answer, "You want to go to London while your brothers are fighting in the heat at the front? When we have rid our country of the Israelis, then you can go to London or even to Tokyo if you wish."

Hakim settled for a motorcycle, which was not shown to me at the time because I was against him riding one, but I did see it in the summer in Alexandria.

I was sitting once with the President and we were talking about Anwar al-Sadat, and he said, "He is very kind and loves us, and he never forgets. He always tells me that he will never forget how well I treated him, and that I sent for him on the day of the Revolution, even though he was not in Cairo. Did you know that he was not part of the Revolution, and that I sent for him?" "Yes, I knew," I said. Anwar al-Sadat was in Rafah at the time the President had sent for him to join the Revolution.

The President traveled to the Soviet Union, and I went to Alexandria with Khaled and Abdel Hakim after they finished their exams. After the President finished his visit to Moscow and before returning to Cairo, he had a medical check-up. The doctors advised him to go to a place close to Moscow, because he had not properly concluded his treatment after his heart attack and he needed a period of rest. Heikal, who had accompanied him on the trip, returned to Cairo before the President and informed me that the President sent me his greetings; he was well and was going to spend two weeks of convalescence in Moscow.

One evening while the President was away, I went out to visit a lady friend. When I returned, the butler told me that Vice President Anwar al-Sadat had passed by to ask about me and the children, but had found no one at home.

I was worried about the health of the President and his stay in Moscow. Heikal's phone call had not put my mind at ease, and so I called Anwar al-Sadat and asked him for news of the President. He told me, "He is fine and in good health. Don't worry."

I remained in Alexandria until the day before the President's arrival from the Soviet Union, when I traveled with the boys back to Cairo. It was a few days before the 23 July celebrations. When the President returned, he told me about his stay in Moscow, which the doctors believed was the only way to make sure he rested. He said, "I asked Heikal to call you so that you wouldn't worry." "He did," I replied.

On 23 July 1970, I sat with the children to listen to the President's speech on television. He congratulated the people of Egypt on the completion of the High Dam. I was not to know that it would be his last Revolution Day speech.

After remaining in Cairo for a few days, the President told me that there was no need to stay in such hot weather and that it would be better to go to Alexandria. He said he would join us in a few days.

The newspapers reported that Anwar al-Sadat was sick with the flu, and when the President came to Alexandria I asked about him and he told me that he was in Alexandria. "Can I go and visit him?" I asked. "If you wish," he replied. The President had already paid him a visit. I decided to go, and found Sadat sitting on his verandah; he welcomed me warmly and I spent a short time with him. The President remained in Alexandria for eleven days, working at his usual pace, then he went back to Cairo and then on to Khartoum for a conference.

I stayed in Alexandria with the children, and when the President was in Cairo he used to call me every day and talk to the children if they were at home. He told me, "I'm alone in Cairo. The house is unbearable without you and the children." I said, "I would be happy to come and be at your side." "No, it's better that you stay in Alexandria. I am out most of the day and come back late at night. You would be alone."

On 1 September, the President traveled to Libya to attend their first revolution celebrations and spent a couple of days there. I went with the children to Cairo to welcome him home on his return and then went back to Alexandria. The President wanted the children to enjoy the sea, and saw no point in us remaining in Cairo while they were still on their summer vacation and he was so busy. He promised to come and spend some time with us in Alexandria.

But the President was not able to come. He had an official visit from the president of Hungary, who was not coming with his wife, so I did not need to be in Cairo to receive him. We returned to Cairo on

12 September. I remember it was a Saturday, because Hakim wanted to spend his last Friday in Alexandria.

MARSA MATRUH

The following day, the President went out to the General Command and came back late as usual.

On Tuesday, the President was leaving Cairo by train for Alexandria, where he would spend the night and then take the train again to Marsa Matruh. He was going to visit the armed forces there, and was taking the defense minister and Hussein al-Shafei with him. The Libyan president, Qaddafi, was going to join them for one day. While we were having lunch, he said, "Would you like to come with me?" I told him I would be happy to go. I had not been since 1953 when he went to convalesce after his appendix operation.

We left Cairo and took Abdel Hakim with us. The President said, "I haven't seen Abdel Hamid for nearly two months. During his holiday I was in Moscow and when I came back he was on an academy trip out at sea, and now I'm leaving Alexandria tomorrow." The defense minister was with us in the salon at the time.

After we arrived at Maamoura, at around nine in the evening, I received a telephone call from Abdel Hamid, "They told me I could leave the academy and come home. I don't want to receive special treatment. This isn't a time for leave, and I don't want to come home now. Did you ask for me?" His voice sounded very upset.

As we were talking, the President came into the room. I told him it was Abdel Hamid on the line and he took the receiver and spoke to him, "I miss you, Mido. As you wish. Do whatever makes you comfortable." When he had said goodbye, I said, "Let him come to see us." The President said, "He's a sensitive boy. The defense minister obviously heard us talking and sent for him." He laughed and went to his room.

A short while later, while the President was on the telephone in the sitting room, I found Abdel Hamid walking in. I embraced him warmly, happy to see my son, and he went in and shook hands with and hugged his father. The President laughed as he said, "You've started smoking. How many cigarettes do you smoke a day? Take care of your health so that when you're older the doctors don't tell you to stop." He continued his telephone conversation with Heikal, telling him how he smelled the smoke on Abdel Hakim; the President had not smoked a single cigarette after being warned by the doctors in July 1968.

We sat down and had dinner together. Abdel Hamid told us that he had refused to leave the academy and then the officer on duty told him that they had orders that he was to leave for the night and he must go. The President asked, "When do you need to get back?" Hamid replied, "They said at ten tomorrow morning, but I want to go back tonight to be with my colleagues when they get up in the morning." "Do as you wish," the President told him. The President went back to his study and Hamid left. It would be the last time he saw his son, the naval academy recruit.

The next afternoon we left by train for Marsa Matruh. Hussein al-Shafei and the defense minister were with us. The minister said, "I called and told them at the academy to give Abdel Hamid leave to go home for the night. When I called back later, they told me he had refused to go . . . and so I told them it was an order." He continued, "Hamid is an exemplary student. He has high morals and a sense of responsibility, and all his teachers praise him highly." The President thanked him.

We arrived at Marsa Matruh at night, amid a warm public welcome as usual. We were taken to the governor's house, where we were going to stay since it was empty at the time. The President decided to take a walk on the beach and asked me to accompany him. We walked to a nearby house where Hussein al-Shafei was residing. He had just come out of the sea when we arrived, and we sat with him for a short while on the terrace.

The following day, the Libyan president arrived with his delegation. They had lunch with the President on the first floor and I lunched with Hakim upstairs. Before they left, the President called for me to meet them.

We stayed for three days while the President visited the armed forces. We then took the train back to Alexandria. On our way back, as we passed through towns and cities, people and their children would come out to greet the President as he was passing. He said, "These are the people I work for." "They look better than before," I said. "I want each and every one of those children to have the same education, health benefit, and general appearance as Khaled, my son. I am not there yet," he said.

The President used to be greatly affected when he saw a young child working as a servant, and would say, "This problem can only be solved gradually. The only solution is to raise the living standards of the farmers in villages and the workers, and to ensure they get an education. God willing, it will end."

THE ARAB SUMMIT CONFERENCE

We remained in Alexandria until 21 September. All the President's time was taken up with his work and following the news of the Palestinians in Jordan.[16] I never saw him rest.

The last two days were spent preparing for the Summit Conference. The President called the Arab leaders and kings by telephone, and told me, "We will leave in the evening." He had heard that morning of the death of his uncle's wife, and he intended that we go and pay our condolences to his cousins before departing, since they lived in Alexandria. We stayed with them for half an hour and then at seven we were on our way to Cairo.

On the way, he received news that President Qaddafi of Libya had arrived in Cairo. When we got home, he told me he was going

---

16 In September 1970, relations between King Hussein of Jordan and the PLO under the leadership of Yasser Arafat erupted in civil war (known as Black September). Nasser organized the Arab Summit in Cairo in September to mediate between the king and the PLO, and a peace agreement resulted.

out to meet with the leaders who had already arrived for the summit. I told him, "It would be better if you rested tonight." He said, "I've already set up the meetings."

We arrived at Manshiyat al-Bakri at around ten. He changed his clothes while I was lying in bed and left, not coming home until after three in the morning. I had witnessed the effort he had exerted all day and could see how exhausted he was.

The following day, Tuesday, he left early in the morning, came back before lunch, and then left again at night, returning after dining with his guests at the Qubba Palace.

On Wednesday, he went out in the morning and stayed out all day with the summit leaders. In the evening, I went and visited a relative of mine who lived in Dokki. I invited her to come back home with me and watch a movie in our cinema. When we got to the house, I found that the President had returned and was in his room. "I was visiting a relative and brought her home with me to watch a movie," I said. "That's good. She'll keep you company," he said, then added, "I'll be staying at the Hilton until the summit is over." He said goodbye and went to the stairs, stopping for a moment to read a small notebook in his hand. Halfway down the stairs, he turned and waved to me again as he sometimes did when I was standing at the top of the stairs. When we had guests in the second-floor salon, he usually went in and greeted the visitor, but this time he did not go in.

The Final Moments

The President stayed at the Hilton, and I followed the news in the papers, on the radio, and on television. On Sunday I was watching the 9 o'clock news, read by Samira al-Kelani. "An agreement has been reached at the Summit Conference. The President bade farewell to some leaders and kings, and the rest will leave Cairo tomorrow." I let out a cry of joy and clapped my hands. My daughter Mona had just come in at that moment and said, "Shall we watch a movie together?" And we went down to the first floor.

At 10:30, the butler came in to tell me that the President had arrived. I told Mona to finish the movie and I went upstairs. I found the President lying in bed and I greeted him warmly, congratulating him on the success of the summit. He had asked for dinner and asked me if I had already eaten. I sat with him as he ate, but he only managed to take yogurt before getting back into bed.

Mona did not finish her movie, but came upstairs, embraced her father, and sat at the edge of the bed. A few moments later Khaled came into the room, and we all sat talking together for a while.

The President was on the phone until after midnight. He said he would get an early night, then in the morning would go and bid farewell to King Faisal and the emir of Kuwait. He put out the lights and slept.

In the morning, he was up before eight. I had already started my day and was waiting for him to call for his breakfast so I could go in and join him. His personal doctor went in first, and then I found the President in front of me, dressed and ready to leave, saying he was going to the airport. I went into his room and found that he had not eaten his breakfast, only a piece of fruit.

The President came back at noon. I was about to go into his room when I found the doctor preparing an ECG. I stepped back and did not go in. Later he left the house again to bid farewell to the emir of Kuwait.

The President came back again at three and I got up to see him. I found Hoda wrapping up, preparing to leave her study and go home. She had been working as his secretary for more than a year. A few months after she had started work, the President had praised the way she did her job and was happy with her.

As I moved toward the bedroom, Hoda whispered to me, "Father seems tired and said he would sleep." The President saw me and called out to me. I went into the room and he waved with his hand for me to sit next to him on the bed. "Have you had lunch, Tahia?" I said, "Yes, I ate with the children." "I won't have lunch today." He beckoned me to stay where I was, which I did for ten minutes while he lay silent on the bed.

Dr. al-Sawy Habib came in and I got up to leave. He told me to fetch the President some juice and I hurried to prepare a glass of lemon and a glass of orange juice, and came back into the room. The President took the orange juice, drank it, and thanked me.

I went and sat in the study, and soon a specialist arrived, Dr. Mansour Fayez. I asked him, "Why are you here, Doctor? When I see you, I know something is wrong with the President, and I worry." He said, "I come every Monday and today is Monday."

I remained in the study. I could hear the President talking and I could hear the news on the radio.

Mona came to me and told me that her father was fine. She took me out of the room and we sat at the dining-room table. The specialist came and said that the President was better and that I could go in and see him, and he lit a cigarette. I said, "I had better not show him I'm worried."

Moments later, Dr. al-Sawy came running, calling for the specialist to join him in the President's room. I got up to go in to the President and Mona prevented me, saying, "Father's fine. Don't worry." And she sat with me in the study. Some time later, two other doctors came; I went into the room and found them around his bed, trying to treat him. I was by that time weeping, and I left the room again so that he would not see my tears, and went and sat in the study. Many of the secretaries came, and then Hussein al-Shafei, and then Heikal, each going into the room and staying there. Everyone who entered the room stayed there, and I sat weeping.

Mona insisted that I go into the sitting room. I walked around in a daze. "Gamal . . . Gamal," is all I could say. I saw the group of people leave the President's room and I rushed in, just as Hussein al-Shafei came out, crying, "It can't be!" Khaled and Abdel Hakim arrived at that moment. They had been out of the house and had no idea what was happening. I found Hoda coming back; she also had no idea of what had happened after she had gone home.

I went into the President's room. I kissed him and wept, then I went out to dress in mourning. I went quickly down to the first floor where I found everyone gathered: the doctors, the secretaries, al-Shafei, Heikal, and Anwar al-Sadat, all standing in the salon.

I told them that I had lived for eighteen years not caring about the Presidency or about being the President's wife. I asked for nothing, only that a place be prepared for me beside him so that I could be near him, and that all I wanted was to rest by his side.

I left and went into the living room. Heikal followed me in and so did Dr. al-Sawy. He asked me to go to my room, and gave me sedatives and stayed by my side. A relative of mine came and stayed with me, and Abdel Hamid arrived from Alexandria. He walked into my room, weeping, "They told me father was unwell and I came by plane." Mona and Hoda came. I was out of touch with time. I tried to get up from the bed. "Where are you going?" asked the doctor. "I am going to lie by his side." Hoda told me, "They have taken him to the Qubba Palace and we went with them." And I said, "It's over. They've taken him!"

Now I am living the third phase of my life, sorrowful and mourning him, and my sorrow has added to my grief. I will mourn him until I rest beside him in the Gamal Abdel Nasser Mosque in Manshiyat al-Bakri, where a resting place has been prepared for me as I wished.

He is Gamal Abdel Nasser, who lived a great man, and he is now in God's care; his history alone bears witness to him.

Index